EVALUATION OF SEXUALLY VIOLENT PREDATORS

BEST PRACTICES IN FORENSIC MENTAL HEALTH ASSESSMENT

Series Editors

Thomas Grisso, Alan M. Goldstein, and Kirk Heilbrun

Series Advisory Board

Paul Appelbaum, Richard Bonnie, and John Monahan

Titles in the Series

Foundations of Forensic Mental Health Assessment, *Kirk Heilbrun, Thomas Grisso, and Alan M. Goldstein*

Criminal Titles

Evaluation of Competence to Stand Trial, *Patricia A. Zapf and Ronald Roesch*

Evaluation of Criminal Responsibility, *Ira K. Packer*

Evaluation of Capacity to Confess, *Alan M. Goldstein and Naomi Goldstein*

Evaluation of Sexually Violent Predators, *Philip H. Witt and Mary Alice Conroy*

Evaluation for Risk of Violence in Adults, *Kirk Heilbrun*

Jury Selection, *Margaret Bull Kovera and Brian L. Cutler*

Evaluation for Capital Sentencing, *Mark D. Cunningham*

Eyewitness Identification, *Brian L. Cutler and Margaret Bull Kovera*

Civil Titles

Evaluation of Capacity to Consent to Treatment, *Scott Y.H. Kim*

Evaluation for Substituted Judgment, *Eric Y. Drogin and Curtis L. Barrett*

Evaluation for Civil Commitment, *Debra Pinals and Douglas Mossman*

Evaluation for Harassment and Discrimination Claims, *William Foote and Jane Goodman-Delahunty*

Evaluation of Workplace Disability, *Lisa D. Piechowski*

Juvenile and Family Titles

Evaluation for Child Custody, *Geri S.W. Fuhrmann*

Evaluation of Juveniles' Competence to Stand Trial, *Ivan Kruh and Thomas Grisso*

Evaluation for Risk of Violence in Juveniles, *Robert Hoge and D.A. Andrews*

Evaluation for Child Protection, *Kathryn Kuehnle, Mary Connell, Karen S. Budd, and Jennifer Clark*

Evaluation for Disposition and Transfer of Juvenile Offenders, *Randall T. Salekin*

EVALUATION OF SEXUALLY VIOLENT PREDATORS

PHILIP H. WITT

MARY ALICE CONROY

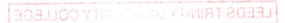
OXFORD
UNIVERSITY PRESS

2009

OXFORD
UNIVERSITY PRESS

Oxford University Press, Inc., publishes works that further
Oxford University's objective of excellence
in research, scholarship, and education.

Oxford New York
Auckland   Cape Town   Dar es Salaam   Hong Kong   Karachi
Kuala Lumpur   Madrid Melbourne   Mexico City   Nairobi
New Delhi   Shanghai   Taipei   Toronto

With offices in
Argentina   Austria   Brazil   Chile   Czech Republic   France Greece
Guatemala   Hungary   Italy   Japan   Poland   Portugal   Singapore
South Korea   Switzerland   Thailand   Turkey   Ukraine   Vietnam

Copyright © 2009 by Oxford University Press, Inc.

Published by Oxford University Press, Inc.
198 Madison Avenue, New York, New York 10016
www.oup.com

Oxford is a registered trademark of Oxford University Press

Library of Congress Cataloging-in-Publication Data

Witt, Philip H.
Evaluation of sexually violent predators / Philip H. Witt, Mary Alice Conroy.
p. ; cm. — (Best practices in forensic mental health assessment)
Includes bibliographical references and index.
ISBN: 978-0-19-532264-4 1. Forensic psychiatry. 2. Sex offenders—Psychology.
[DNLM: 1. Sex Offenses–psychology. 2. Expert Testimony. 3. Forensic
Psychiatry—methods. 4. Risk Assessment. W 795 W827e 2008] I. Conroy, Mary
Alice, 1945- II. Title. III. Series.
RA1151.W59 2008
614'.15—dc22
                                                         2008017355

9 8 7 6 5 4 3 2 1

Printed in the United States of America
on acid-free paper

About Best Practices in Forensic Mental Health Assessment

The recent growth of the fields of forensic psychology and forensic psychiatry has created a need for this book series describing best practices in forensic mental health assessment (FMHA). Forensic evaluations currently are conducted by mental health professionals for a variety of criminal, civil, and juvenile legal questions. The research foundation supporting these assessments has become broader and deeper during recent decades. Consensus has become clearer regarding the recognition of essential requirements for ethical and professional conduct. In the larger context of the current emphasis on "empirically supported" assessment and intervention in psychiatry and psychology, the specialization of FMHA has advanced sufficiently to justify a series devoted to best practices. This series focuses mainly on evaluations conducted by psychologists and psychiatrists, but the fundamentals and principles offered would also apply to evaluations conducted by clinical social workers, psychiatric nurses, and other mental health professionals.

This series describes "best practice" as empirically supported (when the relevant research is available), legally relevant, and consistent with applicable ethical and professional standards. Authors of the books in this series identify the approaches that seem best, while incorporating what is practical and acknowledging that best practice represents a goal to which the forensic clinician should aspire rather than a standard that can always be met. The American Academy of Forensic Psychology assisted the editors in enlisting the consultation of board-certified forensic psychologists specialized in each topic area. Board-certified forensic psychiatrists were also consultants on many of the volumes. Their comments on the manuscripts helped to ensure that the methods described in these volumes represent a generally accepted view of best practice.

The series' authors were selected for their specific expertise in a particular area. At the broadest level, however, certain general principles apply to all types of forensic evaluations. Rather than repeat those fundamental principles in every volume, the series offers them in the first volume, Foundations of Forensic Mental Health Assessment. Reading the first book followed by a specific topical book will provide the reader both the general principles that the specific topic shares with all forensic evaluations and those that are particular to the specific assessment question.

The specific topics of the 19 books were selected by the series editors as the most important and oft-considered areas of forensic assessment conducted by mental health professionals and behavioral scientists. Each of the 19 topical books is organized according to a common template. The authors address the applicable legal context, forensic mental health concepts, and empirical foundations and limits in the "Foundation" part of the book. They then describe preparation for the evaluation, data collection, data interpretation, and report writing and testimony in the "Application" part of the book. This creates a fairly uniform approach to considering these areas across different topics. All authors in this series have attempted to be as concise as possible in addressing best practice in their area. In addition, topical volumes feature elements to make them user-friendly in actual practice. These elements include boxes that highlight especially important information, relevant case law, best-practice guidelines, and cautions against common pitfalls. A glossary of key terms is also provided in each volume. We hope the series will be useful for different groups of individuals. Practicing forensic clinicians will find succinct, current information relevant to their practice. Those who are in training to specialize in forensic mental health assessment (whether in formal training or in the process of respecialization) should find helpful the combination of broadly applicable considerations presented in the first volume together with the more specific aspects of other volumes in the series. Those who teach and supervise trainees can offer these volumes as a guide for practices to which the trainee can aspire. Researchers and scholars interested in FMHA best practice may find researchable ideas, particularly on topics that have received insufficient research attention to date. Judges and attorneys with questions about FMHA best practice will find these books relevant and concise. Clinical and forensic administrators who run agencies, court clinics, and hospitals in which litigants are assessed may also use some of the books in this series to establish expectancies for evaluations performed by professionals in their agencies.

We also anticipate that the 19 specific books in this series will serve as reference works that will help courts and attorneys to evaluate the quality of forensic mental health professionals' evaluations. A word of caution is in order, however. These volumes focus on best practice, not what is minimally acceptable legally or ethically. Courts involved in malpractice litigation, or ethics committees or licensure boards considering complaints, should not expect that materials describing best practice easily or necessarily translate into the minimally acceptable professional conduct that is typically at issue in such proceedings.

The present book focuses on evaluations for civil commitment of Sexually Violent Predators (SVPs). These are the offenders who are determined by the court (through procedures described in this book) to present sufficient risk to the community to justify being detained beyond the expiration of their maximum criminal sentences. Although this book focuses on evaluating SVP cases, the considerations discussed in this book, such as determining a sex offender's risk to reoffend, apply to evaluations of sex offenders in other contexts (e.g., community notification, sentence enhancement, and probationary management) as well. SVP civil commitment cases, and the very commitment procedures associated with them, arouse strong reactions among the lay public, legal professionals, and mental health professionals. Public sentiment, on the one hand, favors longer incarceration for presumably high-risk sex offenders. Civil libertarians, on the other hand, raise concerns about deprivation of the offenders' civil rights and lack of humane conditions. Providing evaluations that are consistent with best practice is both challenging and important in this context.

Kirk Heilbrun
Alan M. Goldstein
Thomas Grisso

Acknowledgments

We thank the series editors, Kirk Heilbrun, Alan Goldstein, and Thomas Grisso, for inviting us to work on this project. We thank Kirk Heilbrun in particular for the many hours he spent editing earlier drafts of the manuscript. His comments have been both helpful and instructive. We also thank our external reviewer, Greg DeClue, for his insightful comments at various stages of the manuscript. Finally, our thanks go to Julia TerMaat, our skilled editor at Oxford University Press, who massaged the manuscript into shape to make it a book.

Contents

FOUNDATION

The Legal Context 1

Sociolegal Purpose and History

Few criminal offenses consistently arouse such strong emotions as sex offenses. Concern about the potential danger of sex offenders to the community has deep historical roots, and there have been many efforts to legislate measures that would in some way reduce sex offender risk. Throughout the decades following the 1930s, many states passed what were then called *sexual psychopath laws* or mentally disordered sex offender laws (Melton, Petrila, Poythress, & Slobogin, 2007). Those sex offenders found to constitute the highest risk to the community—usually described with language emphasizing repeated sex offenses—were eligible for special sentencing provisions, typically involving diversion into a treatment program of indeterminate length (Melton et al., 2007). In some states (e.g., New Jersey), such offenders received indeterminate prison terms in a specialized treatment program. In 1940, the U.S. Supreme Court declared sexual psychopath laws constitutional if applied to "those persons who, by a habitual course of misconduct in sexual matters, have evidenced an utter lack of power to control their sexual impulses and who, as a result, are likely to attack or otherwise inflict injury, loss, pain, or other evil on the object of their uncontrolled and uncontrollable desire" (*State of Minnesota ex rel. Pearson v. Probate Court*, 1940, p. 270).

Beginning in the 1970s, the tide turned, and many of these sexual psychopath laws were repealed. The thinking at that time is perhaps best characterized by the policy finding by a committee of the Group for the Advancement of Psychiatry (GAP), which opined that specialized treatment of sex offenders did not work, implying that specialized sentencing was neither necessary nor beneficial (see discussion in Melton et al., 2007, pp. 280–282).

3

INFO

Sexual psychopath laws were based on four assumptions:

1. Sexual psychopaths are distinguishable from generic sex offenders;

2. individuals commit sexual offenses because of a mental disease;

3. mental diseases are treatable and curable; and

4. mental health professionals can successfully predict which sex offenders are likely to reoffend in the future (Barnickol, 2000, p. 324).

In recent years, partly in response to particularly heinous sexual offenses, legislatures throughout the United States have passed a variety of laws in an attempt to reduce the risk of sexual offending. Some of these laws are statewide in breadth, and focus on notifying the community of sex offenders living in the area. These so-called *Megan's Laws* now exist in every state and the District of Columbia. On a more local level, many municipalities have passed residence restriction laws, preventing sex offenders from living in certain designated areas within the communities, such as within a certain distance of a school.

Legal Contexts for Sex Offender Evaluations

The variety of laws affecting sex offenders has resulted in an equally broad range of legal contexts in which mental health experts can be asked to evaluate sex offenders, and the clinical considerations differ across contexts (see Fig. 1.1).

Pre-adjudication

Frequently, criminal defense attorneys request evaluations after the client has been arrested but well prior to adjudication. Evaluations in these cases require a risk assessment and a treatment plan, particularly as to whether the offender can be managed as an outpatient, a consideration that is relevant when considering if the individual might be suitable for probation. In some cases, if the client is incarcerated

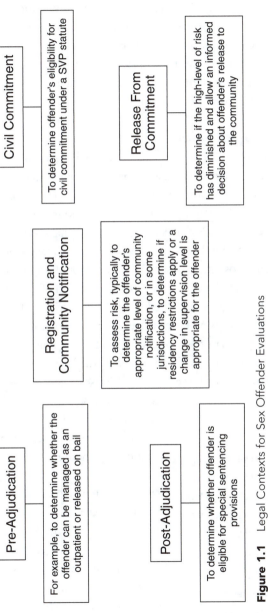

Figure 1.1 Legal Contexts for Sex Offender Evaluations

Pre-Adjudication

For example, to determine whether the offender can be managed as an outpatient or released on bail

Post-Adjudication

To determine whether offender is eligible for special sentencing provisions

Registration and Community Notification

To assess risk, typically to determine the offender's appropriate level of community notification, or in some jurisdictions, to determine if residency restrictions apply or a change in supervision level is appropriate for the offender

Civil Commitment

To determine offender's eligibility for civil commitment under a SVP statute

Release From Commitment

To determine if the high-level of risk has diminished and allow an informed decision about offender's release to the community pending bail, the evaluation may have the more immediate focus of the defendant's risk to public safety if that defendant is released on bail prior to disposition of charges. If the evaluation is favorable, the defense attorney may use the evaluation in an effort to negotiate a more favorable plea for the client. In these informal pre-adjudication cases, no formal statutory guidance is available (although there may be statutory guidelines on releasing defendants on bail, including permissible conditions of bail).

Post-adjudication

In some states (Pennsylvania and New Jersey, for instance), evaluations may be needed after a client has been adjudicated guilty (by plea or conviction) to determine whether he is eligible for special sentencing provisions. In Pennsylvania, offenders found by the court to be *Sexually Violent Predators* can receive an enhanced sentence, up to life. However, Pennsylvania's use of the term "sexually violent predator" is unusual. Most states reserve this term for those sex offenders found eligible for *civil commitment* at the conclusion of their prison sentences, as will be discussed further in the section Eligibility for Civil Commitment. New Jersey requires a psychological evaluation post-plea (or conviction) of sex offenders who have committed certain designated sex offenses before these individuals are sentenced. Defendants found to be repetitive and compulsive sex offenders are eligible for sentencing to a specialized sex offender treatment facility, and their release process is more complex than that for sex offenders sentenced without this finding.

INFO

Megan's Laws

● Refer to sex offender registration and community notification laws in every state and the District of Columbia

● Named after Megan Kanka, the 9-year-old girl who was raped and murdered in New Jersey in 1994

Registration and Community Notification

In every state and the District of Columbia, sex offenders are subject to registration and community notification laws, usually referred to as Megan's Laws. These are named after Megan Kanka, the 9-year-old girl who was raped and murdered in New Jersey in 1994. Although the details of the classification and notification procedures vary from state to state, certain elements are common among them. In New Jersey, for example, a convicted sex offender either living in the community or about to be released from incarceration or residential treatment into the community must be classified as to his level of risk. In New Jersey, this classification is completed by county prosecutors using a risk assessment scale developed by the Attorney General's office (see Witt, DelRusso, Oppenheim, & Ferguson, 1997). The offender's breadth of community notification is dependent on his assessed level of risk. Although the initial risk assessment is completed by county prosecutors, forensic evaluators are regularly retained by both the defense and prosecution to provide expert evaluations and testimony when the offender requests a judicial hearing to challenge his risk level classification.

chapter 1

Evaluations of sex offenders may also occur while the offender is living in the community, either under legal supervision, such as probation, parole, or community supervision for life, or otherwise. These evaluations are sometimes requested to assess risk, typically to determine the offender's appropriate level of community notification. In some jurisdictions, once the offender has been classified for community notification, reclassification is necessary if he relocates to a different community within the state—or sometimes even within the same community. Additionally, some jurisdictions require evaluations and risk assessments to determine whether residency restrictions apply or a change in supervision level is appropriate for that offender. Increasingly, communities are restricting sex offenders' ability to live within proximity to schools; in some jurisdictions, risk assessments may be relevant for these determinations.

Eligibility for Civil Commitment

Also at the time of impending release from incarceration (or from psychiatric hospitalization if found *Not Guilty by Reason of Insanity [NGRI]* or *Incompetent To Stand Trial [IST]* in some jurisdictions), a sex offender may be evaluated to determine his eligibility for civil commitment under a sexually violent predator (SVP) statute. Although the term "SVP" is most widely used, a few states use similar terms (e.g., "sexually dangerous person" or "sexually violent person"). Unlike the pre-sentence and post-sentence evaluations just discussed, SVP evaluations are part of civil, not criminal, proceedings, a point affirmed by the U.S. Supreme Court in both *Kansas v. Hendricks* (1997) and *Kansas v. Crane* (2002). However, the civil nature of SVP commitments is still controversial. As Monahan notes, "For the commentators, the 'civil' designation of the sexually violent predator statute at issue in *Hendricks* and *Crane* was a legislative pretext to circumvent constitutional concerns regarding double jeopardy and the ex post facto application of law" (2006, p. 433). SVP commitment evaluations constitute the primary focus of this book and will be discussed in detail later.

Consideration for Release From an SVP Facility

Finally, evaluations also occur when an offender who has been civilly committed under an SVP statute is considered for release from the SVP facility. The challenge in these evaluations is to determine whether the high level of risk that presumably led to the offender's SVP commitment has diminished, and to what extent, allowing an informed decision about his release to the community (Witt & Barone, 2007). Evaluators have the difficult task of determining whether changes in *dynamic risk factors,* perhaps resulting from changes in personal attributes or progress in treatment, outweigh *static risk factors,* such as characteristics of criminal history.

Evaluative Frameworks

A variety of evaluative frameworks are used in different jurisdictions and for different legal contexts. In New Jersey, to determine whether a convicted sex offender is eligible for *special "repetitive-compulsive" sentencing* after conviction, that individual is evaluated at a specialized state correctional facility by mental health professionals employed by the state. In Pennsylvania, to determine whether a sex offender is eligible for enhanced sentencing, he is evaluated by an individual serving on a board of appointed professionals. In some jurisdictions, risk assessments for community notification are completed by individuals who are not mental health professionals, such as by county prosecutors in New Jersey. Some jurisdictions (for example, New Jersey) require a psychiatrist to make the final recommendation to the court as to whether a sex offender is eligible for SVP commitment. In this instance, the underlying philosophy is that SVP commitment is simply another form of civil commitment and, therefore, the purview of physicians. Other jurisdictions allow psychologists to perform such evaluations and make such recommendations to the court.

SVP Civil Commitment Statutes

The first SVP civil commitment statute was passed in Washington State in 1990 (*Washington Laws* § 71.09.020, 1990). As is typical with new sex offender statutes, Washington's SVP commitment statute was passed in response to a heinous sex offense. In this instance, in 1987, Earl Shriner was released from prison in Washington after having served his maximum term. While incarcerated, he had reportedly informed other inmates of his plans to rape and torture children after his release. Although Washington authorities had attempted to civilly commit him upon his release, they were unsuccessful because he was not found to be mentally ill. Two years after his release, he sexually assaulted and castrated a young boy, leaving the boy for dead after the assault (LaFond, 2005). One year later, Washington passed its SVP statute.

As of 2003, over 2,500 individuals had been committed under SVP statutes (Miller, Amenta, & Conroy, 2005). In July 2006, the federal government enacted the Adam Walsh Child Protection and Safety Act of 2006, and Title III of this act empowers the Federal Bureau of Prisons to pursue the civil commitment of sex offenders under circumstances and using procedures analogous to those used by the states.

Differences Between Traditional Civil Commitment and SVP Commitment

There are some characteristic differences between traditional civil commitment laws and SVP commitment laws. Among the most prominent are the following:

- SVP commitments do not require a recent overt act; traditional civil commitments usually do.

INFO

Presently, 18 states and the District of Columbia have SVP commitment laws: Arizona, California, Florida, Illinois, Iowa, Kansas, Massachusetts, Minnesota, Missouri, New Hampshire, New Jersey, North Dakota, South Carolina, Tennessee, Texas, Virginia, Washington, and Wisconsin.

- SVP commitments occur after an offender has served his term of incarceration, whereas traditional civil commitments typically occur instead of incarceration.

- SVP commitments do not usually involve diagnoses of psychosis, whereas traditional civil commitments frequently involve such diagnoses.

- SVP civil commitments require an assessment of *volitional impairment*, whereas traditional civil commitments do not.

Specifics of State Statutes

SVP statutes in all states, with the exception of Texas, involve inpatient commitments; currently, Texas is the only state with an outpatient SVP commitment statute. All states, with the exception of California, allow indeterminate SVP commitments, with California's SVP statute providing a renewable 2-year commitment (Lieb, 2003). All states have periodic review procedures once an individual has been committed under an SVP statute, ranging from 6 months to every 2 years (Sreenivasan, Weinberger, & Garrick, 2003).

Legal Standards

Certain elements are common to SVP civil commitment statutes across jurisdictions. A typical SVP statute is that enacted in 1994 in Kansas (*Kansas Stat. Ann.* § 59–29a02, 2003), which defines a Sexually Violent Predator as "any person who has been convicted of or charged with a sexually violent offense and who suffers from a mental abnormality or personality disorder which makes the person likely to engage in the predatory acts of sexual violence." Two of the three primary elements of SVP statutes (to be discussed in detail in Chapter 2) are evident in the Kansas statute: (1) some form of *mental abnormality*, (2) resulting in the individual being more likely to commit future sex offenses.

INFO

SVP Statutes

Primary elements:

- Mental abnormality
- Risk of future sex offenses
- Volitional impairment

Other possible elements:

- Juvenile delinquency
- Incompetency

The third element, volitional impairment, is implicit, and was later articulated through case law, as will be discussed subsequently.

Some jurisdictions also allow a finding of delinquency for juveniles who have committed sex offenses as the offense foundation. Almost all jurisdictions allow a finding of NGRI or incompetency for a sex offense charge to serve as this offense foundation. For example, the New Jersey statute encompasses these possibilities by defining a Sexually Violent Predator as follows:

> A person convicted, adjudicated delinquent or found not guilty by reason of insanity of a sexually violent offense, or who has been charged with a sexually violent offense but found incompetent to stand trial, and suffers from a mental abnormality or personality disorder that makes the person likely to engage in acts of sexual violence if not confined in a secure facility for control, care, and treatment. (*New Jersey Stat. Ann.* § 30:4–27.26(b))

The reader will notice that New Jersey's statute differs from Kansas's in that it offers two additional bases for "mental disorder"— an NGRI or an IST finding. However, unlike Kansas's statute, New Jersey's statute does not include those merely "charged with a sexually violent offense." There is considerable variability among jurisdictions on points such as these, although we have no clear explanation for this variability.

Kansas v. Hendricks

The first SVP commitment in Kansas was of Leroy Hendricks. This case led to a major challenge to the constitutionality of SVP commitment laws in *Kansas v. Hendricks* (1997). Kansas filed the first SVP petition against Hendricks, an offender who had molested at least ten children before he was convicted and sentenced to 10 years in prison. Shortly before his scheduled release, the state of Kansas sought his civil commitment as an SVP. After a jury found Hendricks to qualify for commitment under Kansas's SVP statute, he began a series of legal challenges, which eventually were resolved in the U.S. Supreme Court. On June 23, 1997, the U.S. Supreme Court, in a 5-to-4 decision, upheld the constitutionality of the Kansas SVP statute. The Court reached majority findings in two areas relevant to forensic SVP

CASE LAW
Kansas v. Hendricks (1997)

- The U.S. Supreme Court upheld the constitutionality of the Kansas SVP statute and

  1. articulated the links between mental abnormality, volitional impairment, and risk, and

  2. established that SVP commitment does not constitute double jeopardy.

- All states follow the Kansas statute as a model.

evaluations. First, the Court concluded that the Kansas statute's use of the term "mental abnormality" did not violate due process requirements. The Court concluded that in Hendricks's case, his diagnosis of pedophilia was a valid condition that impaired his volitional control and thereby made him likely to commit future offenses (*Kansas v. Hendricks*, 1997, p. 360). The *Hendricks* decision provides a clear articulation of the links between the required legal elements in SVP evaluations: A mental abnormality (broadly defined) causes volitional impairment that in turn makes it likely that the individual will commit another sex offense if released into the community.

Hendricks also raised another legal issue: whether an SVP commitment constitutes *double jeopardy*—that is, punishing him twice for the same crime. The Court's findings on this point are summarized by Amenta (2005):

> [T]he Supreme Court found that because the Act established a *civil*, not a *criminal* proceeding, its intent was not punitive in nature. It suggested five qualities of the proceedings rendered them civil in nature (*Kansas v. Hendricks*, 1997): (a) the employment of strict procedural safeguards; (b) the failure to implicate the two objectives of punishment: deterrence and retribution; (c) commitment is made on the basis of a mental abnormality or personality disorder, not criminal intent; (d) the individual subject to commitment is afforded the status of a civil committee and provided treatment if it is available; and finally, (e) immediate release is permitted when the committee can show he or she is no longer dangerous and disordered. (p. 11)

CASE LAW

Seling v. Young (2001)

- The U.S. Supreme Court upheld the Washington SVP statute as both civil and constitutional, but found that the adequacy of care and treatment of those committed could be challenged in court.

Following the *Hendricks* decision, additional states have enacted SVP commitment statutes. Although there are minor variations in wording, all states follow the Kansas statute as a model, given that the U.S. Supreme Court found that statute to be constitutional.

Seling v. Young

In *Seling v. Young* (2001), an individual committed under the Washington State SVP statute challenged the law, contending that even if the statute itself was constitutional (as found in *Hendricks* while the *Seling* case was pending before the appellate court), it was unconstitutional as applied to him. He contended that no effective or individualized treatment was available to him, so, in practice, the law was simply a punitive extension of his incarceration. The U.S. Supreme Court held that the statute itself was both civil and constitutional, regardless of its implementation in any given case. However, the Court found that an individual committed under the law still must have adequate care and treatment, and the adequacy of such care and treatment could be challenged in court.

Kansas v. Crane

Perhaps the most controversial aspect of SVP statutes is the requirement that volitional impairment be found. As will be discussed in Chapters 2 and 3, there is considerable debate even within the mental health community as to whether volitional impairment can be reliably assessed. Moreover, there is little legal guidance on this point. One widely cited case on this point is another Kansas case, *Kansas v. Crane* (2002). The U.S. Supreme Court, in interpreting its prior finding in

CASE LAW

Kansas v. Crane (2002)

- The U.S. Supreme Court found that volitional impairment need only be serious, not total, for civil commitment requirements.

- It did not clarify, however, the required extent of volitional impairment or how to determine this.

Hendricks, found "no requirement of complete or total lack of control" (*Kansas v. Crane,* 2002, p. 411). The volitional impairment need only be serious (*Kansas v. Crane,* 2002, p. 413). Although the court was helpful in clarifying that the volitional impairment need not be complete, it was less helpful in articulating just how much volitional impairment is needed to meet the threshold or how one can determine whether such volitional impairment is present. In later chapters, we will suggest some guidelines in evaluating this component and discuss more fully the debate over whether it can be assessed reliably at all.

Admissibility of Evidence Regarding Risk Assessment

Another issue that came frequently before the courts, at least in the early days of SVP commitment hearings, involved the nature of the evidence that was admissible regarding risk assessment. Early on, there was considerable controversy over the admissibility of actuarial sex offender risk assessment scales. Some states follow the *Frye* standard (*Frye v. United States,* 1923) regarding the admissibility of scientific or expert evidence. *Frye* jurisdictions focus most on general acceptance in the field of the kind of evidence presented in the immediate case. In *Daubert* (*Daubert v. Merrell Dow Pharmaceuticals, Inc.,* 1993) jurisdictions, the judge acts as a scientific gatekeeper, ruling on whether the evidence meets standards of scientific acceptability based on criteria such as whether the form of evidence has been peer reviewed and whether it has an acceptable error rate. (See comparison of *Frye* and *Daubert* standards in Table 1.1.)

Hearings have been held on the admissibility of risk assessment evidence in both *Daubert* and *Frye* jurisdictions. For example, in the case *In re Commitment of R.S.* (2001), the appellate court in New Jersey (a *Frye* state) ruled in favor of the admissibility of the results of *actuarial instruments* in assessing sex offender risk. The court cited other jurisdictions having done the same, and general agreement by experts that the instruments were accepted in the field. The following year, the New Jersey Supreme Court upheld this appellate court decision, concluding that results of actuarial risk assessment

Table 1.1 │ Frye Standard vs. Daubert Standard

Frye v. United States (1923)	Daubert v. Merrell Dow Pharmaceuticals (1993)
• Based admissibility of evidence on general acceptance in the field	• Based admissibility of evidence on standards of scientific acceptability • Judge plays a more active role in assessing whether evidence meets scientific criteria

instruments were admissible in SVP commitment proceedings when such evidence was combined with other factors and did not constitute the only information relied on by experts (*In re Commitment of R. S.,* 2002).

Similarly, in the state of Washington, the state appellate court (*In re Detention of Broten,* 2003) held that the trial court did not violate Federal Rule of Evidence 403 in admitting actuarial tools into evidence, because such instruments had been used for many years and were determined to produce reliable results. Monahan (2006) reviewed court decisions in a number of jurisdictions admitting actuarial and otherwise structured risk assessment procedures, and noted, "In the past several years, however, a number of violence risk assessment tools have become available, and courts as well as legislatures have become remarkably receptive to their introduction in evidence" (pp. 408–409, footnotes omitted).

However, this legal acceptance of actuarial instruments has not been universal (see, for example, *Illinois v. Taylor,* 2002), and the evaluator should determine what methods are accepted in her state. In fact, Rogers and Shuman (2005, p. 342) note that the pattern of acceptance of actuarial instruments is "uneven from state to state and even within the

CASE LAW

In re Commitment of R.S. (2002)

● New Jersey Supreme Court upheld the admissibility of the results of actuarial instruments in assessing sex offender risk based on *Frye* standards.

borders of the same state." Consequently, evaluators should be aware of admissibility of any specialized assessment instruments within their jurisdictions and be prepared for cross-examination on the empirical foundations of those instruments.

Issues Regarding Scales

Some issues involving scales' definitions and relative predictive ability have not yet been clarified. For example, for a scale to be considered actuarial, must scale contents be derived through an empirical process, such as that used to develop the Static-99 (Hanson & Thornton, 1999)? Many scales that were originally constructed through *rational methods,* in contrast to *empirical methods,* later have been the subject of predictive validity studies, and the results have generally been as robust as those for scales constructed solely by actuarial means. A good example is the SVR-20 (Boer, Hart, Kropp, & Webster, 1997). Although this scale is considered a form of structured professional judgment, having been constructed through a rational review of the literature, its predictive validity (when scored following mechanistic scoring rules), when the Area Under the Curve in a Receiver Operating Characteristics analysis is examined, differs little from that for those scales constructed by actuarial means, such as the Static-99 (Douglas, 2007). Moreover, this scale development process is modeled after traditional test development methods, involving initial rational analysis followed by internal and external validity studies. Perhaps the most critical aspect is not how the items were selected. Regardless of how the items were selected (whether by statistical means through a meta-analysis or through a rational review of the literature), the degree to which the instrument consistently improves the ability to predict future sex offending or increases the ability to manage the offender's risk is the key issue. In the following chapters we will discuss these distinctions between risk assessment methods further, in a more detailed presentation of the use of actuarial scales. In the end, it may matter less how a scale was constructed; what matters more is whether it is reliable and valid.

Legal Procedures

Although there are variations in legal procedures among the various jurisdictions, there are certain elements common to most of them. When an incarcerated sex offender is nearing his release date from prison, a brief screening is usually performed by institutional staff. If that screening indicates that the inmate may meet criteria for SVP civil commitment, a more comprehensive evaluation is then conducted by mental health staff. Those inmates who are found to meet criteria for SVP commitment—involving presence of a mental abnormality that would cause volitional impairment, resulting in a likelihood of reoffending—are then referred to the state agency responsible for handling SVP commitments. This legal agency would then file a motion (or petition) for SVP commitment. In some jurisdictions, the inmate is temporarily committed pending a full commitment hearing.

In any event, within a statutorily defined time, a full commitment hearing is held, and the court determines whether the individual, in some cases by then no longer a prison inmate, meets the criteria for SVP commitment. During the hearing, expert mental health testimony may be heard from both defense and state experts, sometimes solely by the state's experts and sometimes with rebuttal testimony by the experts of the individual being considered for SVP commitment. The SVP commitment hearings may be either a bench or jury trial, depending on the jurisdiction. These SVP commitment proceedings are civil, although they have some of the characteristics of criminal proceedings. In addition, the burden of proof is on the state, although the level of proof required varies among jurisdictions— either clear and convincing (as is the case in non-SVP civil commitment proceedings) or beyond a reasonable doubt, again depending on the jurisdiction. The federal SVP proceedings require clear and convincing proof in a non-jury hearing. In SVP proceedings, there is no protection against self-incrimination in most jurisdictions (with the exception of a few states, to be discussed later in Chapter 5), as there is in criminal proceedings.

Once committed under an SVP statute, the individual has periodic reviews to determine his suitability for release (see Fig. 1.2).

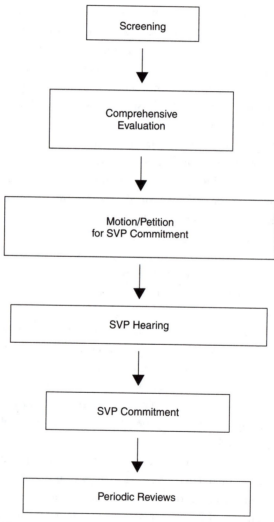

Figure 1.2 Legal Procedures

Forensic Mental Health Concepts | 2

For decades, forensic mental health experts have struggled with the gap between mental health constructs and legal constructs. Although the two types of constructs may sound similar, there is frequently not a direct correspondence between them. The two families of constructs have different roots and traditions. Legal constructs are the result of legislated statutes and interpreted case law. Mental health constructs flow from medical and behavioral science theory and validating research. Constructs in both areas evolve over time.

The difficulty in fit between legal and mental health constructs is evident in virtually all areas of forensic mental health assessment. For example, two legal standards for insanity are in common use among the states—M'Naghten and American Law Institute (ALI)—the former being a narrow cognitive standard and the latter including volitional impairment. Words descriptive of mental, intellectual, and behavioral functioning are used in these insanity standards—for example, "knowing" in the cognitive aspect of the M'Naghten standard and "appreciation" in the cognitive aspect of the ALI standard. Their definitions, however, do not arise from mental health theory or research. Rather, these terms have been placed in statutes by legislatures; over the years, mental health professionals have attempted to approximate these constructs through reviewing legal analysis in the area and developing instruments and procedures to assess domains believed to reflect these constructs (see discussion in Borum, 2003). Although many people found not guilty by reason of insanity are diagnosed with a psychotic disorder, such a diagnosis does not necessarily result in an individual's meeting the legal criteria for insanity. In fact, this diagnosis is not legally required for a finding of insanity. Similar difficulties arise in the criteria for SVP commitments.

INFO

There are three interrelated forensic mental health constructs relevant in SVP evaluations:

1. Mental disorder or abnormality

2. Volitional impairment

3. Risk

SVP commitment statutes vary in their specificity of factors to be considered in an evaluation or, in some statutes, of what instruments must be used (see summary in Miller, Amenta, and Conroy, 2005, p. 30). For example, Virginia's statute is explicit in requiring administration of the Rapid Risk Assessment for Sexual Offense Recidivism (RRASOR; Hanson, 1997) or a comparable instrument. The California statute requires consideration of criminal and psychosexual history; type, degree, and duration of sexual deviance; and severity of mental disorder. Texas requires an evaluation of *psychopathy*, but allows the evaluator to choose the evaluation method.

Constructs Defining Mental Disorder or Abnormality

All SVP laws require some form of mental abnormality as a foundation. (For a detailed description of statutory language for the various elements of SVP laws, see Miller et al., 2005, or Sreenivasan, Weinberger, & Garrick, 2003.) Of the 18 states that have SVP commitment laws, 13 use the following wording: "A congenital or acquired condition affecting the emotional or volitional capacity that predisposes the person to the commission of criminal sexual acts to a degree constituting the person a menace to the health and safety of others" (Sreenivasan et al., 2003, p. 473). It is difficult to imagine a condition that is not either congenital or acquired, a point made by Doren (2002) in his text on the subject. Each state then has further language defining the mental abnormality, with some states (e.g., New Jersey) explicitly including a personality disorder in their definitions. This inclusion of an Axis II disorder as classified in the *Diagnostic and Statistical Manual of Mental Disorders, Fourth Edition, Text Revision* (*DSM-IV-TR*; American Psychiatric Association, 2000) as a qualification for civil commitment is one of the more controversial aspects of SVP commitment laws. In traditional civil commitments, an Axis I diagnosis, typically a psychotic disorder, is most often the mental

BEWARE
There is controversy over using an Axis II diagnosis as a qualification for SVP civil commitment.

condition at issue. It would be unusual for a traditional civil commitment (that is, a non-SVP civil commitment) to be made solely on the basis of an Axis II diagnosis. Consequently, use of an Axis II diagnosis (most commonly *antisocial personality disorder*) for an SVP civil commitment has generated considerable debate in the field.

Certain elements are evident in the language just referenced.

1. First, "mental disorder" is defined broadly. There is no language ruling out any specific diagnosis (even on Axis II), and there is no language requiring a specific diagnosis from the *DSM-IV-TR* (Sreenivasan et al., 2003). In fact, there is no requirement that a *DSM* diagnosis even be given, although that is frequently done.

2. Second, there must be a connection between the mental condition and emotional or volitional impairment. The inclusion of volitional impairment, in particular, makes the legal criterion diverge from traditional *DSM* diagnoses.

3. Third, the emotional or volitional impairment must predispose the individual to commit sex offenses, although the extent of this predisposition is not specified.

DSM Diagnoses

As noted earlier, a *DSM* diagnosis is not required by statute. Moreover, as Rogers and Shuman note, "No diagnosis can be automatically equated with the SVP standard" (2005, p. 346). Doren comments further on significant problems with *DSM* diagnoses in SVP cases:

> [T]he unfortunate reality is that the DSM-IV often leaves the clinician without sufficient guidance for diagnostic situations common to incarcerated sex offenders. As a group, these offenders bring their own unique characteristics and circumstances to diagnostic scrutiny, characteristics that the DSM-IV often delineates too ambiguously or not at all. (2002, p. 54)

In practice, evaluators routinely include *DSM* diagnoses and base their findings for mental abnormality on this diagnosis. One primary purpose of diagnosis is to facilitate clear communication among professionals regarding an individual's mental condition and symptoms (Doren, 2002), and the *DSM-IV-TR* is the de facto standard for such diagnoses. For this reason, SVP commitment evaluators frequently spend considerable effort providing a *DSM* diagnosis as a foundation for their SVP commitment findings.

Axis I Diagnoses

The Axis I diagnosis found most often among SVP commitment cases is some form of *paraphilia* (Doren, 2002; Levenson, 2004b). The elements of a paraphilia, in *DSM-IV-TR*, are as follows:

1. Intense sexually arousing fantasies, sexual urges, or behaviors involving

2. nonhuman objects, the suffering or humiliation of one's partner, or children or other nonconsenting persons

3. that occur over a period of at least 6 months, and

4. these urges, fantasies or behavior cause the individual marked distress or functional impairment (American Psychiatric Association, 2000, p. 566).

Doren (2002) notes a number of definitional problems with these criteria. First, it is unclear what the *DSM-IV-TR* means by the word "child." Although a diagnosis of *pedophilia* requires a sexual focus on prepubescent individuals, what of individuals who engage in sex with individuals who are postpubertal (perhaps 14 or 15 years old, or even younger, with an adolescent who has entered puberty early) but below the age of consent in the relevant jurisdiction? If one is diagnosing paraphilia NOS for an individual who engages in sex with postpubertal individuals below the age of legal consent, as is frequently the case, the evaluator must be clear about how he is defining the word "child," given that cross-examination on this issue is likely. Moreover, given that sexual

INFO

In SVP cases, three Axis I diagnoses are of particular interest:

●   pedophilia

●   sexual sadism

●   paraphilia not otherwise specified (NOS)

attraction to postpubescent adolescents is not necessarily abnormal (e.g., Freund & Costell, 1970), a diagnosis of paraphilia for a person who acts on such attraction must be carefully scrutinized.

Second, for a diagnosis of paraphilia, the *DSM-IV-TR* specifies evidence that the deviant urges, fantasies, or behavior must have occurred over a period of at least 6 months. If the individual has demonstrated illegal sexual behavior spanning at least 6 months, there is no difficulty with this criterion, but this is not always the case. In some instances, the individual will have committed an offense spree—high-frequency illegal sexual behavior spanning less than 6 months. In other cases, the individual will have a few widely spaced offenses, with no intervening repetitive offenses.

In the application of any *DSM* diagnoses, evaluators should keep in mind that the book itself includes the caution that "specific diagnostic criteria included in the *DSM-IV* are meant to serve as guidelines to be informed by clinical judgment and not meant to be used in a cookbook fashion" (American Psychiatric Association, 2000, p. xxxii). There is a tendency on the part of attorneys to attempt to interpret *DSM* criteria as though they are statutory. In other words, attorneys may wish to imply that if a particular individual's difficulties do not exactly match the *DSM* criteria, then a diagnosis cannot be made. However, the introduction to the *DSM-IV-TR* itself makes clear that this is not the intent, and attorneys should be disabused of this notion.

PARAPHILIA AND RAPE

An individual who sexually assaults other adults presents particular diagnostic challenges, given that there is no *DSM* paraphilia category for rape. A commonly used solution is to diagnose such individuals as paraphilia NOS, nonconsent. However, not all rapists are paraphiliacs. Some commit rape out of a broadly antisocial or psychopathic personality or lifestyle, which will be discussed later in this chapter (see section Psychopathy). Moreover, there is the difficulty of inferring sexual arousal to nonconsenting sexual interactions in the absence of an admission of such by the individual. Such minimization of deviant sexual arousal is common among sex offenders of all

BEST PRACTICE
Use clinical judgment when diagnosing, and remind attorneys that *DSM* criteria are guidelines only.

types, but with rapists, it presents particular diagnostic difficulties, given that their sexual choice—another adult—is not illegal or deviant. Doren (2002) describes a number of useful indicators of paraphilia NOS, nonconsent under circumstances when the offender does not report deviant sexual arousal:

- Ejaculation or clear signs of sexual arousal during events that are clearly nonconsensual
- Repetitive patterns of action, as if following scripts
- Virtually all the person's criminal behavior is sexual
- Raping when the victim had already been willing to have consensual sex
- Raping under circumstances with a high likelihood of being caught
- Having concomitant cooperative sexual partners, but sexually offending nonetheless
- Broad range of rape victim types
- Maintenance of a "rape kit," or set of paraphernalia to assist in the commission of rapes

Although Doren focuses this description on rapists, some of these criteria are useful in assessing the extent or presence of volitional impairment among sex offenders generally. This will be discussed in the next section.

RELIABILITY OF DIAGNOSES

There has been debate in the field regarding the reliability of *DSM* diagnoses generally and paraphilia diagnoses specifically. Levenson (2004a) found low reliability (using kappa coefficients) of diagnoses used in SVP commitments, and her work has been cited (e.g., Campbell, 1999, 2004) to suggest the unreliability of such diagnoses. However, Packard and Levenson (2006) have reanalyzed the Levenson (2004a) data and concluded that reliance on kappa is misleading in this context, as many statistical assumptions for computing kappa coefficients are not present in the sample. Packard and Levenson (2006) found, in fact, that interrater agreement in the majority of cases led to paradoxically low kappa values. They also concluded that use of other measures of interrater agreement, such as overall percentage of diagnostic agreement or agreement on commitment recommendation, led to relatively high levels of interrater reliability. Suffice it to say, this issue is not yet resolved.

Although some investigators (e.g., Rogers, 2001; Rogers & Shuman, 2005) recommend the use of structured interviews to establish *DSM* diagnoses, anecdotal evidence suggests that such structured interviews are used infrequently by SVP evaluators. No such structured interviews exist for the most frequently diagnosed Axis I disorder—paraphilia (Miller et al., 2005). Moreover, as Miller et al. (2005) note, although the criteria for pedophilia changed from the *DSM-III* to *DSM-IV*, and the criteria for paraphilia changed from the *DSM-IV* to *DSM-IV-TR*, little research has been conducted on these altered diagnoses, either during the field trials or otherwise. Finally, as Miller et al. (2005) note, there is the unresolved question of whether pedophilia can go into remission, given that often an SVP evaluator will be diagnosing pedophilia (or a related paraphilia) from historical information, related to the sexual offender's behavior prior to a lengthy incarceration.

Axis II Diagnoses

The Axis II diagnosis most often found among SVP commitment cases is a long-standing pattern of antisocial behavior, beginning in adolescence or earlier, and involving a pervasive disregard for the rights of others, codified in the *DSM* diagnosis of antisocial personality disorder (APD). A study by Levenson (2004b) in Florida found that in a sample of moderate- to high-risk sex offenders (N = 450), almost half of those referred for SVP commitment had a diagnosis of APD, compared with less than 20% of the sex offenders not referred for SVP commitment. A review of SVP civil commitment cases in Texas found APD to be among the most common diagnoses (Miller et al., 2005). Similarly, a study in Arizona of 120 male SVP civil commitment cases found 77% to have at least one personality disorder diagnosis, with personality disorder NOS (42%) and APD (40%) being the most common (Becker, Stinson, Tromp, & Messer, 2003). A recent study in Texas (Amenta, 2005) also found APD to be the most common *DSM* diagnosis on either Axis I or Axis II, with 46% of the SVP commitment cases having been so diagnosed.

QUESTIONS FOR THE DIAGNOSIS OF APD

Doren (2002) noted a number of relevant questions concerning the diagnosis of APD in sexual offenders. The SVP evaluator would be well advised to consider these issues as part of the evaluation and prepare for them on cross-examination. These issues include the following:

- *Presence of a conduct disorder before age 15.* For a diagnosis of APD, the *DSM-IV-TR* indicates that the individual must show the onset of a conduct disorder by age 15. However, the *DSM-IV-TR* is unclear as to whether an actual diagnosis of conduct disorder is required or whether *evidence* of such a disorder is sufficient. It is probably the latter, given the difficulties involved in eliciting the full criteria for a conduct disorder diagnosis years after the fact. However, the SVP evaluator should be prepared to defend this position under cross-examination, given the ambiguity of the *DSM-IV-TR* on this point.

- *Good institutional behavior.* A skilled attorney will sometimes note that an otherwise antisocial SVP client has behaved well while incarcerated, thus presumably casting doubt on the diagnosis of APD, which requires persistent violation of others' rights. This issue is particularly acute with SVP candidates, many of whom have committed numerous crimes and consequently spent much time incarcerated. The evaluator who diagnoses such an individual with APD should note the increased structure associated with incarceration, and the concomitant decreased likelihood for antisocial behavior under those circumstances. Doren reasonably suggests that "actions exhibited in the general community should be given more weight" (2002, p. 89).

INFO

Antisocial personality disorder involves

- a long-standing pattern of antisocial behavior, beginning in adolescence or earlier, and

- a pervasive disregard for the rights of others.

- *Lack of information regarding juvenile history.* At times, there is no information available regarding an SVP candidate's juvenile history. Thus, there are no grounds for even finding *evidence* of a conduct disorder, particularly if the individual does not acknowledge a history of delinquency. When there is no relevant information on behavior during adolescence that is associated with a diagnosis of APD, Doren suggests that a diagnosis of APD is not indicated—although an alternative diagnosis of personality disorder NOS, with antisocial features may be a suitable substitute. A diagnosis of personality disorder NOS, with antisocial features has no specific requirement of adolescent antisocial behavior, but in effect and practice appears to be used as shorthand for "likely antisocial personality disorder, but not able to delineate all the diagnostic criteria."

ISSUES REGARDING APD DIAGNOSES

Beyond the technical issues with evaluation methods and cross-examination concerning APD, we have broader concerns on this issue. First, the literature indicates that a majority of prison inmates in general—up to 40%–60% in one study (Moran, 1999), 50%–70% in another (Hare, 1998), and 49%–80% in a third (Cunningham & Reidy, 1998)—will qualify for a diagnosis of APD. Yet, relatively few general-prison inmates will commit future sex offenses. Consequently, a diagnosis of APD would have poor discriminant validity if the question of who will commit a future sexual offense were asked of all those with this diagnosis, rather than those at a priori higher risk (such as individuals already convicted of at least one sexual offense). To our knowledge, no studies have yet been conducted to determine the extent to which a diagnosis of APD is related to sex offending in a population that has already committed one sex offense (although such work has been done with those found to meet the criteria for psychopathy, as we will discuss in Chapter 3).

Second, unlike Axis I disorders, which frequently have some biological basis and typically respond to medication, Axis II diagnoses are more shorthand ways of summarizing long-term behavior patterns. All too often we have seen how Axis II diagnoses develop a life of their own, almost as if they were evidence of an alien invading and possessing the personality of the so-diagnosed individual.

Finally, as even the *DSM-IV-TR* states, "The specific diagnostic criteria included in the DSM-IV are meant to serve as guidelines to be informed by clinical judgment and are not meant to be used in a cookbook fashion" (American Psychiatric Association, 2000, p. xxxii). The evaluator should remember this caution when tempted to rely too mechanistically on the diagnostic criteria in the *DSM-IV-TR*.

Psychopathy

One non-*DSM* personality disorder frequently considered is psychopathy. There is confusion among professionals between APD and psychopathy, with some equating the two. In fact, the *DSM-IV-TR* itself is misleading on this point, indicating that "[t]his pattern [APD] has been referred to as psychopathy, sociopathy, or dissocial personality disorder" (American Psychiatric Association, 2000, p. 702). However, the criteria for psychopathy are more extensive, yielding a smaller number who meet these full criteria than those for APD. The group diagnosed with psychopathy overlaps with that diagnosed with APD. For instance, within male forensic populations, psychopathy has a 15% to 25% base rate (Hare, 1998), whereas APD has a much higher base rate, with estimates ranging from 40%–60% (Moran, 1999) to 50%–70% (Hare, 1998).

The standard method of assessing psychopathy is the Psychopathy Checklist—Revised (PCL-R) (Hare, 2003). In general, higher levels of psychopathy are associated with higher levels of both sexual and general recidivism (see review in Barbaree, 2005). This structured rating scale has two broad factors, a callous, egocentric personality style (Factor 1) and an impulsive, antisocial lifestyle (Factor 2), which combine to yield a total score. The PCL-R has 20 items, each

INFO

States vary in their use of psychopathy in SVP proceedings. For example, in Texas, consideration of psychopathy is required by statute; in California, it is mandated by written policy (California Department of Mental Health, 2004). Consideration of psychopathy is customary, but not required, in New Jersey.

scored 0, 1, or 2. Hare (2003) indicates that a cutting score of 30 is required for a diagnosis of psychopathy, and this is generally followed. However, some research suggests that a lower cutting score can result in accurate classification of psychopathy (Quinsey, Harris, Rice, & Cormier, 1998). It may be that future modifications of the PCL-R will offer different levels of categorization, given recent empirical evidence (e.g., Edens, Marcus, Lilienfeld, & Poythress, 2006; Marcus, John, & Edens, 2004; Walters, Duncan, & Mitchell-Perez, 2007; Walters, Gray, et al., 2007) that psychopathy may have more than two (present vs. absent) categories.

Constructs Defining Volitional Impairment

It is not sufficient for a sex offender to suffer a mental abnormality; to be eligible for an SVP commitment, the mental abnormality must cause volitional impairment as well. In *Kansas v. Hendricks* (1997), the majority concluded that volitional impairment narrowed the class of individuals subject to SVP civil commitment sufficiently to legitimize that procedure. In *Kansas v. Hendricks* (1997), the U.S. Supreme Court noted 17 times that mental abnormality must be linked to an offender's serious difficulty controlling dangerous sexual behavior (Miller et al., 2005). In fact, the inclusion of volitional impairment as a requirement for civil commitment in *Hendricks* was novel. Previously, civil commitment required only mental disease or defect (broadly defined in SVP statutes as mental abnormality), as a result of which the person's release would create a substantial risk of bodily injury to another person or serious damage to property (Sarkar, 2003). There is no explicit statutory or case law requirement in traditional civil commitment proceedings that volitional impairment be present or assessed.

However, this is an area of law in which there is ongoing debate. Justices Scalia and Thomas, in their dissent in *Kansas v. Crane,* opined that the Kansas statute does not require a separate determination of volitional impairment; rather, in their opinion, the Kansas statute presumes that if mental abnormality causes a likelihood of repeated illegal sexual behavior, then that link is sufficient to establish volitional impairment. Consequently, the forensic evaluator should be alert for future nuanced changes in statutes or case law on the issue of volitional impairment.

Lack of Consensus

Perhaps no issue in SVP evaluations is more hotly debated among both mental health and legal professionals than how (or even whether) to assess and reach an opinion on volitional impairment. LaFond has written, "There is virtually unanimous consensus that MHPs [mental health professionals] cannot determine when an individual has significant difficulty controlling his behavior" (2005, p. 140). Similarly, Miller and colleagues (2005) observe, "Not only is there no method developed by which to assess behavioral control, there is no clear definition of what is being measured. Any standard would appear more normative than scientific" (p. 42). Perhaps the concerns of the field regarding the construct of volitional impairment can be best captured by the widely quoted statement of the American Psychiatric Association, here referring to the volitional prong of the insanity defense: "[T]he line between an irresistible impulse and an impulse not resisted is probably no sharper than that between twilight and dusk" (1983, p. 685).

In *Kansas v. Crane* (2002) the U.S. Supreme Court opined that such volitional impairment did not need to be absolute, only serious. The *Crane* Court clarified its prior *Hendricks* finding on volitional impairment as follows:

> In recognizing that fact, we did not give to the phrase lack of control a particularly narrow or technical meaning. And we recognize that in cases where lack of control is at issue, inability to control behavior will not be demonstrable with mathematical precision. It is enough to say that there must be proof of serious difficulty in controlling behavior. And this, when viewed in light of such features of the case as the nature of the psychiatric diagnosis, and the severity of the mental abnormality itself, must be sufficient to distinguish the dangerous sexual offender whose serious mental illness, abnormality, or disorder subjects him to civil commitment from the dangerous but typical recidivist convicted in an ordinary criminal case. (2002, p. 413)

BEWARE
Be alert for future nuanced changes in statutes or case law on the issue of volitional impairment.

As Justices Scalia and Thomas wrote in their dissent in *Crane,* the Court gives little guidance on the specific criteria or circumstances that can be used to assess the extent of volitional impairment. In fact, the majority in *Crane* explicitly declined to provide a standard for determining volitional impairment, stating, "safeguards of human liberty in the area of mental illness and the law are not always best enforced through precise bright-line rules" (2002, p. 407).

Consequently, the evaluator is faced with little clarity on the extent and nature of volitional impairment to be assessed in SVP cases. First, it is unclear whether the individual must be more volitionally impaired than the average adult or than the average sex offender (Miller et al., 2005). Second, although it may be possible to agree in extreme cases—those that display either overwhelming volitional impairment or relatively little—what of all the cases in between? Without a clear articulation of what is meant by "serious," this determination becomes difficult and potentially unreliable.

Offering an Opinion

Given such concerns among mental health experts regarding opinions on volitional impairment, why would an SVP evaluator provide one? First, LaFond's earlier comment notwithstanding, there is no unanimous agreement on whether SVP evaluators should offer such opinions. Both *Hendricks* and *Crane* require that such a determination be made before an individual is committed through an SVP statute. If an SVP evaluator is to offer an opinion on the issue of commitment, then it seems necessary that the evaluator assess the components of commitment, one of which is volitional impairment.

The evaluator should weigh the pros and cons of offering both an *ultimate legal opinion* and a more specific opinion on the controversial penultimate question of whether the individual suffers from volitional impairment. If the evaluator does offer an opinion regarding volitional impairment, there are certain guiding principles, which we will review below. However, as noted above, the evaluator should be aware that these guidelines are based on rational or theoretical analysis more than empirical studies.

BEWARE Note that guidelines for offering an opinion regarding volitional impairment are based on rational or theoretical analysis more than on empirical studies.

Court Decisions Regarding Volitional Impairment

Mercado, Schopp, and Bornstein (2005) reviewed a series of court decisions from Minnesota, which they proposed "bring clarity to the idea of lack of volitional control" (p. 298). Although these court decisions are specific to one jurisdiction, they do reflect how some courts are beginning to articulate the parameters defining volitional impairment. Mercado et al. (2005) summarized court decisions offering the following on volitional impairment:

- There is no requirement that the impairment be caused by an extreme cognitive deficit resulting from conditions such as severe mental retardation, dementia, or organic brain damage, or psychosis, sleep walking, or seizures.

- Planning or grooming behavior does not necessarily preclude a finding of volitional impairment, although such planning may be one factor potentially inconsistent with such a finding.

- Lack of insight into one's behavior may indicate volitional impairment.

- Loss of control may be situational, may result from removal of external controls, and need not be present all the time.

- Repeated illegal conduct despite consequences or fear of capture is relevant.

- Loss of control may be present even when the offender has entrenched beliefs that justify sexual contact with minors.

Characteristics Consistent With Volitional Impairment

A number of authorities have suggested characteristics consistent with a finding of volitional impairment. These characteristics follow the common theme of an inability of the individual to desist from illegal sexual behavior despite negative personal consequences.

FOUR AREAS OF CONSIDERATION

Rogers and Shuman (2005) proposed four areas to be considered:

1. *Lack of capacity for meaningful choice:* Does the behavior have a driven quality? In contrast, was there evidence of rational consideration of choices?

2. *Disregard for personal consequences:* Does the behavior occur or continue despite negative personal consequences for the individual? In contrast, is there evidence of attempts to minimize the consequences of the actions, such as avoiding detection?

3. *Incapacity for delay:* Was the individual unable to delay sexual gratification for lengthy periods? Is there evidence of opportunity-seeking behavior by the individual?

4. *Chronicity:* Is the behavior enduring? Does the behavior consist of more than a few isolated instances?

2
chapter

TWO DIMENSIONS FOR ANALYSIS

Doren (2002) proposed that volitional impairment can be analyzed along two dimensions. First, he suggested that chronic sex offending can be a reflection of the individual's impaired ability to learn from experience—in this case, the experience of repeated negative consequences of sex offending. The difficulty of learning from experience, Doren suggested, can be the result of a personality disorder, thus tying the impaired ability to avoid negative consequences to a mental disorder. This first explanation provides an avenue for an Axis II cause of volitional impairment.

However, we offer two cautions with regard to this Axis II explanation. First, as we noted earlier, some personality disorders, such as APD, for the most part are no more than behavioral descriptors absent known pathology or etiology (Conroy, 2003). The presence of such Axis II characteristics (or diagnosis) may make it statistically more likely that an individual will recidivate, but no more than that. Second, reasoning from the presence of a broad Axis II disorder to the presence or absence of functional capacities without going through careful consideration of the individual's characteristics would be using a *nomothetic* approach entirely, to the exclusion of *idiographic* considerations—not

BEWARE
Volitional impairment cannot be implied solely on the presence of an Axis II disorder such as APD.

an approach that we recommend. Consequently, the evaluator should avoid viewing Axis II disorders as distinct entities with great explanatory power.

Doren (2002) also proposed that in some cases, the individual has a limited view of his choices. For example, the paraphilic individual may see illegal sexual behavior consistent with his paraphilia as the only satisfying means of sexual gratification. This second explanation provides an avenue for an Axis I cause of volitional impairment. By way of example, Doren (2002) states:

> [T]he person's desire for sexual contact with children and/or violence is sufficiently strong that it overwhelms the individual's ability to consider various options and consequences. The strength of this desire, although not "irresistible" (to borrow an old legal concept, from the phrase "irresistible impulse") becomes the basis for his deciding to sacrifice concerns for the consequences of his actions to himself and others. It is not the desire per se that is the problem, but the strength of the desire relative to other actively considered options. (p. 17)

FOUR INDICATIVE FACTORS

In a recent article, Mercado, Bornstein, and Schopp (2006) suggested that a review of case law and (limited) empirical studies reveals four factors that indicate volitional impairment:

- Verbalized lack of control
- History of sexual crimes
- Lack of offense planning
- Substance use

Although the above factors were generally found in case law, and to some extent in the limited prior studies, not all were supported in Mercado et al.'s (2006) own survey. In this study, Mercado et al. surveyed 159 participants comprising three groups: 43 legal professionals (both judges and attorneys), 40 psychologists, and 76 jury-eligible undergraduates. They found verbalized inability to control conduct and a history of pedophilic behavior to be significantly related to a rating of having volitional impairment, but found no such effect for planning or substance use.

Case Law

Although we strongly encourage the evaluator to know the legal context generally, we caution against allowing a review of case law (or statutory law, for that matter) in her jurisdiction to draw the evaluator too far afield from her area of competence. If the forensic evaluator does offer an opinion on a jurisdiction-specific construct, the specific statutory and case law language of the construct should be considered. Often, reading the relevant case law for the jurisdiction will guide the forensic evaluator on the nuances of interpretation of the construct in that jurisdiction. For example, Mercado et al. (2005) summarized a series of case decisions in Minnesota regarding volitional impairment. Evaluators in other jurisdictions can conduct similar analyses of case law in their own jurisdictions to gain perspective on what considerations the courts consider relevant and salient.

2
chapter

Psychophysiological Research

Miller and colleagues (2005) point to psychophysiological research that has shown promise in explaining loss of behavioral control. They reviewed a variety of studies that have found evidence that neurological deficits underlie loss of behavioral controls. The loss of behavioral control may be caused by disorders such as mental retardation or frontal lobe lesions, commonly believed to be associated with neurological impairment. They also reviewed a number of studies that have found neuropsychological correlates of psychopathy, suggesting a relationship between this kind of personality disorder and neurophysiological abnormality. However, Miller et al. add that neuropsychological disorders are not often used as the basis for sex offender commitments, primarily because these disorders rarely address the type of behavior involved in SVP evaluations (e.g., grooming, planning—that is, behavior that does not reflect instantaneous impulsivity).

Constructs Defining Risk

The last of the three constructs relevant to SVP evaluations relates to whether the person is likely to engage in sexual violence as a result of mental abnormality or personality disorder. It is the increased likelihood of future proscribed or dangerous behavior (caused by mental illness, in traditional civil commitment cases) that has historically been the hallmark of civil commitment. As the widely modeled Kansas statute puts it, the mental abnormality and resulting volitional impairment must lead to the offender's becoming "likely to engage in repeat acts of sexual violence" (*Kansas Stat. Ann.* § 59–29a01, 2003 & Supp. 2004).

The words "likely to engage" immediately point to a forward-looking assessment of risk of future sex offending, or "sexual violence," in the Kansas statute. Over the past few decades, the field has made considerable progress in performing such forward-looking risk assessments, particularly through the construction and use of structured, empirically based risk assessment instruments. As Monahan (2006) notes, civil commitment procedures make no assumption that all individuals with mental illness or mental abnormality will be dangerous. Rather, the assumption is that evaluators will have some means for accurately distinguishing between those individuals whose mental abnormality makes them dangerous and those whose mental abnormality does not make them dangerous.

The commonly used phrase "likely to commit" was clarified to some extent in *Kansas v. Crane* (2002), in which the Court indicated, "the person's propensity to commit acts of sexual violence is of such a degree as to pose a menace to the health and safety of others" (p. 288). However, there is still variation between jurisdictions as to how likely the risk of future sexual violence must be to meet the threshold for SVP commitment. Case law among the states has proposed a variety of "clarifying" phrases (see table and related discussion in Sreenivasan et al., 2003, pp. 477–478), such as "highly likely," "probable," and "highly probable." Missouri's "more likely than not" is perhaps the clearest. However, Missouri is the exception in that regard, given that courts have generally rejected or reached contradictory findings (see Rogers & Shuman, 2005; Sreenivasan et al., 2003) on a definition of "likelihood." In many jurisdictions, "likely" is simply left undefined.

Doren (2002) summarizes the lack of clarity or agreement on defining "likely" among the various states:

> Some people interpret the term as synonymous with "more likely than not." Others make the interpretation using the term "probable" (an interpretation made by the Florida Supreme Court, for

instance), which is by no means necessarily equated with "more likely than not." Still others say the term "likely" varies in its meaning depending on the degree of injury that would be expected to a victim. For instance, the percentage "likelihood" needed for commitment for someone who kills his victims is viewed as significantly lower than for someone who "only" touches children's buttocks over their clothes. A fourth interpretation consistently views "likely" as metaphorically the degree of likelihood for an airplane crashing when you would no longer get on the plane, a figure quite regularly conceived as significantly below "more likely than not." (p. 20)

The SVP evaluator needs to determine what standard for "likelihood" or "propensity" is being used in her jurisdiction. Doren (2002) reasonably suggests consultation with other evaluators in the same state to reach, if possible, a consensus on a definition of "likely" in that jurisdiction. Although it may not be possible to reach an exact definition through such consensus, at least a normative (one hopes reasonable) definition can be reached, specific to the statute and case law in that state. However, the evaluator should bear in mind that even a definition agreed upon by a consensus of evaluators may be found lacking by a judge or jury, in which case the "consensus" will need to be revised. In the end, this is an "ultimate issue" matter, best decided by the court. One suggestion is to limit one's conclusion and testimony through avoiding an opinion on the ultimate issue of whether the individual qualifies as an SVP. Rather, the evaluator can articulate as precisely as possible about the offender's likelihood of a new sex offense, leaving it for the court to determine whether that level of likelihood meets the court's definition of "likely." Forensic evaluators frequently struggle to determine how much likelihood is enough, when this determination may well lie outside their purview.

Risk Assessment Methods

To assess this increased likelihood of future sex offending, SVP evaluators engage in what is perhaps the most thoroughly researched area of these evaluations—risk assessment. Historically, mental health evaluators first relied on unstructured clinical judgment to assess risk of future

BEWARE The meaning of "likely" in regards to risk may vary in different jurisdictions and contexts. A definition may be determined by consensus, but may be better left to the court as an "ultimate issue" matter.

BEWARE
Unstructured
clinical judg-
ments are poor predictors
of future dangerousness.

dangerousness (broadly defined). Decades of research on risk assessment accuracy have found that such unstructured clinical judgments are poor predictors of future dangerousness. In a widely cited work, Monahan (1981) reviewed early research on this area and found that, using unstructured clinical judgment, mental health professionals were wrong more often than right in predicting future violence in institutionalized mental patients. As Monahan (2006, pp. 406–407) succinctly states, "Little has transpired in the intervening decades to increase confidence in the ability of psychologists or psychiatrists, using their unstructured clinical judgment, to accurately assess violence risk." Few SVP evaluators evaluate risk using only unstructured clinical judgment.

Most SVP evaluators use a structured instrument that has an empirical relationship to risk of future sexual offending (Miller et al., 2005). Given the agreement that structured, empirically based risk assessment approaches are the most accurate, these are the approaches recommended here. At this time, there is some debate in the field as to which of the empirically guided structured methods is best, with some evaluators favoring an *actuarial approach* and others favoring a structured clinical judgment approach. However, there is no literature or authority that recommends unstructured clinical judgment. There are three variants of this empirically directed approach (Doren, 2002):

- *Research guided:* This approach uses risk and protective factors gleaned from the empirical literature, typically compiled into a coherent structured guide. The guide developers conduct a rational analysis of the empirical literature to select the risk and protective criteria. Although guides based on this method may not have originally been validated through predictive studies, many have later been subject to such studies, making them sometimes difficult to distinguish from actuarial scales, discussed next. If the research-guided methods are scored in a mechanistic, rule-based manner, the distinction between research-guided and actuarial methods becomes even more blurred. Examples of research-guided methods with varying degrees of

empirical relationship to sex offending include the
Sexual Violence Risk—20 (SVR-20; Boer, Hart, Kropp,
& Webster, 1997), the HCR-20 (Webster, Douglas,
Eaves, & Hart, 1997), and the Psychopathy
Checklist—Revised (PCL-R; Hare, 1991).

- *Actuarial:* Two characteristics define the actuarial
approach, according to Doren. The first is that the risk
(and rarely, protective) criteria are selected on the basis
of ability of each criterion to predict future sex
offending, usually through analyzing pooled groups of
studies, termed "meta-analytic studies." Second, the
rules for combining and scoring the criteria are mechanistic and must be followed without deviation.
Examples of actuarial scales are the Static-99 (Hanson &
Thornton, 1999, 2000) and the Sex Offender Risk
Appraisal Guide (SORAG; Qunisey, Harris, Rice, &
Cormier, 1998, 2006). Actuarial instruments give
heavy weight to static, historical variables, focusing on
assessing the individual's risk at a given time, what is
termed (Douglas & Skeem, 2005) "risk status."

- *Clinically adjusted actuarial:* As Doren explains, this
procedure involves using an actuarial approach as the
foundation, but adjusting these results under some
circumstances. Anecdotal evidence indicates that this
approach is widely followed among SVP evaluators. It
has its pros and cons. The obvious disadvantage is that
deviating from the mechanistic scoring rules of an
actuarial scale may decrease the predictive ability of the
evaluator (Campbell, 2004) or that at least the accuracy
of clinically adjusting an actuarial scale is unknown. The
advantages include the tailoring of the evaluation to the
specific circumstances of the offender, as well as the
inclusion by the evaluator of dynamic risk and protective
factors. This issue is as yet unresolved. However, a
recent study by Knight and Thornton (2007) indicates
that addition of dynamic risk information to static risk
information can enhance the accuracy of prediction.

BEWARE
Adjustment of the score or category of an actuarial tool, rather than interpretation of the data, is problematic.

Although there is considerable discussion in the literature regarding *clinically adjusted actuarial* methods and, in fact, this is the commonly used term, we believe this term actually reflects a conceptual confusion about two aspects of risk assessment: results and interpretation. If the evaluator adjusts an actuarially derived score or category by somehow changing it, this is problematic. This method would interweave actuarial prediction and unstructured clinical judgment, as evaluators do not know how much to change a score or category. However, a forensic evaluator is responsible for the interpretation of all of his results, using all sources of data. This evaluator might use an actuarial tool that yielded a "low" risk for future sexual offending, but indicate that, for specified reasons, the risk is somewhat higher than "low." In all honesty, the evaluator should add that he does not know how much higher than "low" the risk is. We advocate that actuarial tools be used in the manner in which they were developed, but interpreted in the context of all sources of information, that information being clearly specified by the forensic evaluator. This is no different from the way in which a forensic evaluator uses any piece of information. After all, one does not say that one has clinically adjusted a Minnesota Multiphasic Personality Inverntory-2 (MMPI-2; Butcher, Dahlstrom, Graham, Tellegen, & Kaemmer, 1989); one simply says that the MMPI-2 was interpreted using all available information to do so. The same holds true for actuarial risk assessment scales. In this way, the conceptual confusion regarding how actuarial results can be "adjusted" is clarified.

Another way of conceptualizing risk assessment methods has been proposed by Douglas (2007). He divides risk assessment methods into three types: clinical, actuarial, and structured professional judgment (SPJ). He then considers three stages in each—data review, data coding, and data analysis—and notes whether each process is structured (through use of explicit decision rules) or unstructured. This is best represented in Table 2.1.

Criticism of Risk Assessment Scales

Although, in practice, an opinion on the increased likelihood of future sex offending is anchored in an offender's score on some form of structured risk assessment scale, the use of such scales has its

Table 2.1 | Types and Stages of Assessment

	Data Review	Date Coding	Data Analysis
Clinical	No	No	No
Actuarial	Yes	Yes	Yes
SPJ	Yes	Yes	No

Source: Courtesy of Douglas (2007)

critics. Campbell (2004), who is perhaps the most prominent critic of the use of these scales in SVP proceedings, offers the following criticisms:

- Methods based on structured clinical judgment are not sufficiently standardized, reliable, or validated to meet scientific standards. Campbell also notes the lack of an explicit method of converting findings from structured clinical judgment methods to recidivism risk rate.

- Campbell suggests that actuarial methods are not sufficiently comprehensive (focusing primarily on static, historical risk factors), that the scoring manuals are insufficient, and that "field" reliability (in contrast to "research" reliability) has not been established. He also proposes that actuarial methods have insufficient classification accuracy when taking into account the relatively low base rate of sex offender recidivism (thus increasing the likelihood of false positive findings).

It is unclear the extent to which such criticisms of research-guided risk assessment scales with SVP evaluations are influenced by the intense criticisms of SVP statutes and procedures generally. Evaluators should be familiar with Campbell's cautions and should carefully consider each statement in their reports and testimony as to whether they can state their conclusions with "reasonable certainty" or "reasonable psychological certainty," the usual terms of art in testimony. Although the debate in this area is likely to continue, a reasonable position seems to be that adopted by Monahan (2006), who recommends that disagreement over the substantive merits of sexually violent predator statutes not cause evaluators and decision makers to discard empirically validated assessment tools, which can "effectuate their statutory goals" (p. 523).

Empirical Foundations and Limits | 3

The SVP Population

Although a great deal of the empirical research on this population has treated sexual offenders as though they comprise a homogeneous group, it is misleading to do so. Would one expect the opportunistic rapist who commits rapes while burglarizing homes to closely resemble the school choir master who is an upstanding citizen—except that he has molested dozens of boys in his choir? Is it likely that the 19-year-old who has sex with his 15-year-old girlfriend has the same personality profile as the middle-aged alcoholic who rapes strangers late at night while intoxicated? Would a man who forces nonconsensual sex on his fiancée in a fit of anger be apt to respond to the same treatment as one who has molested his elementary-school-age daughter regularly over several years? Despite the general application of the label "sex offender," it has become virtually axiomatic that this is an extremely heterogeneous group (Hoberman, 1999; Knight, Rosenberg, & Schneider, 1985; Prentky & Burgess, 2000).

In 1999, Bumby and Maddox surveyed judges and found that 47.6% of them believed mental health professionals could produce a valid profile of a sex offender. Although some efforts have been made to develop taxonomies (Knight, Carter, & Prentky, 1989; Prentky & Burgess, 2000), research has not yielded any profile specific to sex offenders, nor has it produced a subcategory of sex offenders (Conroy, 2003). It is not uncommon for courts to ask if a particular defendant fits the test profile (e.g., the Minnesota Multiphasic Personality Inventory-2, or MMPI-2) of a sex offender. However, no MMPI-2 profile has been found to differentiate sex offenders from other offenders or from non-offenders (Becker & Murphy,

1998; Levin & Stava, 1987; Murphy & Peters, 1992). Taxonomies of sex offenders have been developed, but these taxonomies classify known sex offenders. They are not useful in determining whether an alleged sex offender has committed an offense.

If studies do subdivide sex offenders into categories, the most common groupings are rapists and child molesters. (Some also include a category of noncontact sexual offenders such as those engaged in voyeurism. However, these are unlikely to be the subject of SVP proceedings and will not be considered in this volume.) For our purposes, we will look at the following subgroups of sex offenders: rapists, child molesters, incest offenders, and juveniles.

Rapists

Some attempts have been made to categorize rapists in terms of psychopathology. However, other than for the disorders of substance abuse and antisocial personality disorder, it is relatively rare for rapists to meet criteria for a significant mental disorder (Conroy, 2003). In addition, the diagnosis of antisocial personality disorder is so common among incarcerated individuals, sex offender and otherwise, as to have little discriminating power. Researchers generally do not find more than 15% of rapists suffering from psychotic disorders, even when subjects are taken from prisons and psychiatric hospitals (Lalumiere, Harris, Quinsey, & Rice, 2005). Although there is some evidence that the general criminal population is more likely to have minor neurological abnormalities than the rest of society, there is no evidence of structural brain abnormalities specific to sexual aggression (Lalumiere et al., 2005).

Others have attempted to subdivide rapists by their motivation for the crime. During the 1970s, *Groth's Typology* was developed, featuring the dimensions of power and anger as the primary categories (Groth, Burgess, & Holmstrom, 1977). More recently, the Massachusetts Treatment Center Classification System for Rapists (Version 3) classified rapists' primary motivations as opportunistic, pervasively angry, sadistic, nonsadistic, and vindictive; groups were then subdivided by social competence (Prentky & Burgess, 2000). Although theoretically interesting and perhaps promising for purposes of treatment development, these classification systems have had little impact on the assessment of SVPs. This is probably because they do not directly address diagnosis, volitional impairment, or risk. In addition, to date, other than the initial research to derive these classification systems, relatively little research has focused on these systems.

Child Molesters

In classifying child molesters, the most common categorizations attempt to separate those who suffer from pedophilia from non-pedophiles, and those who are exclusively attracted to children from those who also have adult partners. However, the application of the diagnosis of pedophilia, as defined in the *Diagnostic and Statistical Manual* (fourth edition, text revision) (*DSM-IV-TR*, American Psychiatric Association, 2000), remains somewhat nebulous (Miller, Amenta, & Conroy, 2005) for reasons discussed in detail in Chapter 2. The diagnosis is generally made by either history or use of a *phallometric measure*. If history is used, it often becomes simply a behavioral description, unless the subject admits to urges and fantasies. Attorneys frequently treat the *DSM-IV-TR* criteria as though they were statutory—either the person has molested a child or children over at least a 6-month period or he has not. The most common phallometric measure is the *penile plethysmograph*; however, research has indicated some difficulties with both generalizability of techniques and the potential for faking (Miller et al., 2005). This makes it difficult to establish a diagnosis in a valid and reliable manner. Alternatively, Knight and colleagues (1989) developed the Massachusetts Treatment Center Child Molester Typology (MTC:CM3), which subtypes these offenders by level of fixation, social competence, and degree of contact with children. However, this system has seen little application relative to recidivism risk.

Although there has been concern over whether the individual is exclusively attracted to children, little attention has been paid to that group of child molesters whose criminal history is exclusive to sexual offending with children. Criminal lifestyle has been found to be very important in assessing risk for recidivism among sex offenders in general (Hanson & Bussiere, 1998). One study examining the Psychopathy Checklist—Revised (PCL-R) scores of child molesters who were not criminally versatile suggested that this group may have some unique characteristics (Bauer, 2006). Specifically, exclusive child molesters did score significantly lower on the PCL-R than more criminally diverse groups of offenders.

Incest Offenders

Research has distinguished extrafamilial from intrafamilial child molesters and generally found that incest offenders have lower rates of reoffending than those who offend against nonfamily members (Greenberg, Bradford, Firestone, & Curry, 2000; Hanson, 2002). However, these data are often viewed with some skepticism, given the likelihood that incest is underreported, compared with reporting of offenses committed by strangers or acquaintances. For child molesters generally, deviant arousal has been found to be a primary predictor of recidivism (Hanson & Bussiere, 1998). Among incest offenders, however, some investigators have reported less deviant responses (Frenzel & Lang, 1989). In other studies, erectile response has been found to be nondiscriminating for adult preference pattern (Barbaree & Marshall, 1989) or to be deviant but unrelated to recidivism (Firestone et al., 1999).

Mixed Offenders

There is also a group of offenders who victimize both adults and children. Some research would suggest this is a very small group, and that offenders are generally stable in their choice of victims (Guay, Proulx, Cusson, & Ouiment, 2001). However, when self-report is used with some promise of confidentiality, it appears that a good number of offenders may have victims of all ages (Abel, Becker, Cunningham-Rathner, Mittelman, & Rouleau, 1988; Weinrott & Saylor, 1991). Unfortunately, anyone claiming a mixture of victims is often excluded from research studies, so very little substantive data have been reported. In addition, given that this research is entirely self-report, we would not recommend placing a heavy weight on it.

Females

There has been little research on female sexual offenders. Based on what is known, it would appear that findings on adult male offenders often do not apply to female offenders. Females seem more likely to offend against relatives, have fewer sexual partners, are less apt to have prior legal problems, are more likely to have a prosocial history, and are more likely to seek therapy (Vandiver & Walker, 2002). They are also more likely than male offenders to have symptoms of a mental illness (Johansson-Love & Fremouw, 2006; Lewis & Stanley, 2000), but less likely to be diagnosed with a paraphilia (Allen, 1991). Women are also more likely to have come from abusive family backgrounds (Christianson & Thyer, 2003; Hislop, 2001).

Juveniles

In recent years, attempts have been made to focus on juvenile sex offenders as a separate population. As with adults, juvenile sexual offenders tend to be very heterogeneous and may be even more undifferentiated in regard to victim selection (Wijk et al., 2006). Juvenile offenders tend to be less specialized than adults, with subsequent crimes less likely to be sexual in nature (Rasmussen, 1999). They are also more likely to have been sexually abused sometime during childhood (Becker & Hunter, 1997). Otherwise, few generalizations can be made. Although juveniles are among the least likely to be subjects of an SVP evaluation, in the occasional SVP case, evaluators are asked to assess an adult who committed sexual offenses as a juvenile and has been incarcerated ever since. In such cases, evaluators should be familiar with the literature on sexual recidivism by juvenile offenders.

3
chapter

Diagnosing a Disorder

In *Kansas v. Hendricks* (1997), the U.S. Supreme Court made it very clear that a "mental disorder" need not be drawn from the *DSM*. However, clinicians typically use recognized diagnostic categories, and the Association for the Treatment of Sexual Abusers (ATSA) endorses this practice (Association for the Treatment of Sexual Abusers, 1997). There is general agreement that, with the exception of a paraphilia or substance abuse disorder, significant Axis I disorders in this population are rare (Barbaree & Marshall, 1998; Hanson & Bussiere, 1998).

BEWARE Although it is important to be familiar with the general research on the sex offender population, it may not provide sufficient information relevant to the single individual. The population is too heterogeneous and the subtyping, to date, too broad. Hence, although the nomothetic research is useful as a general guide, additional idiographic analysis may be warranted.

INFO

There are generally three elements that need to be addressed in SVP forensic mental health assessment (FMHA):

1. whether the individual has the requisite disorder;

2. whether that disorder somehow impairs the individual's ability to control behavior; and

3. the nature of the subsequent risk to society.

Methods of evaluating each element will be described in turn in this chapter.

Diagnoses most commonly used to support SVP civil commitments have been either paraphilias or personality disorders (Conroy, 2003; Miller et al., 2005).

Paraphilia

Some (e.g., Becker & Murphy, 1998) have argued that a paraphilia is the most appropriate diagnosis, given the nature of SVP civil commitment. However, it has also been argued that there are little or no empirical data on the validity or reliability of any of the paraphilic diagnoses (Miller et al., 2005). O'Donohue, Regev, and Hagstrom (2000) have noted that the changes in criteria for the paraphilias made between 1994 and 2000 were not grounded in any actual data or formal measurement. Under *DSM-IV-TR* criteria, one can be diagnosed with a paraphilia if one simply acts on one's aberrant sexual urges with a nonconsenting partner over a specified period of time. Beyond that, evaluators may be inconsistent in determining who merits such a label.

For example, some clinicians would say that the act of rape merits the diagnosis of paraphilia NOS, whereas others contend that, despite *DSM* content, a clinical diagnosis must be more than a description of behavior. Legal experts have criticized the mental health community

INFO

A *DSM* diagnosis is not required but is commonly used, particularly paraphilia and antisocial personality disorder.

for putting forth "scientific" diagnoses that anyone who is privy to adequate records and speaks the English language could reach (Schopp, Scalora, & Pearce, 1999).

Personality Disorder

The courts have historically had difficulty grappling with the concept of personality disorder. Although personality disorders alone rarely form the basis for more traditional civil commitments, the legal system has seemed to embrace these constructs in the commitment of sex offenders. Not surprisingly, antisocial personality disorder (APD) is seen most often. For example, in Texas, APD was among the most commonly used diagnoses in these proceedings (Texas Department of Criminal Justice Programs and Services Division, 2002). Researchers have found antisocial traits to be quite common among sex offenders, particularly rapists (Firestone, Bradford, Greenberg, & Serran, 2000). However, the use of APD as the requisite mental abnormality for civil commitment may be casting too wide a net. Between 40% and 80% of male prison inmates have been found to qualify for that diagnosis (Cunningham & Reidy, 1998; Hare, 1998; Moran, 1999).

Psychopathy

Even though not formally included in the *DSM*, the personality disorder of psychopathy has proven to be a much more important consideration in SVP evaluations than APD. *Psychopathy*, as used in this volume, refers to the personality construct first developed by Cleckley, more recently researched by Hare and colleagues, and most accurately assessed using the PCL-R (Hare, 2003). In contrast to the very high rates of APD noted among incarcerated male felons, psychopathy has been found in less than 25% of this population (Cunningham & Reidy, 1998). Researchers have repeatedly found high scores on the PCL-R linked to both violent and sexual recidivism (Barbaree, Seto, Langton, & Peacock, 2001; Hanson & Bussiere, 1998; Hanson & Morton-Bourgon, 2004; Harris, Rice, & Quinsey, 1998; Hildebrand, 2004; Langton, Barbaree, Harkins, & Peacock, 2006; Quinsey, Lalumiere, Rice, & Harris, 1995; Serin, Mailloux, & Malcolm, 2001; Seto & Barbaree, 1999). Therefore, the PCL-R can be an extremely useful tool for SVP evaluators to consider. If an individual scores high in

INFO

High scores in psychopathy have been linked to increased risk for reoffense.

psychopathy, the person would likely be at higher risk for reoffending. However, a low score would only mean that psychopathy is one risk factor that the individual does not have. In psychometric terms, psychopathy has considerable sensitivity, but little specificity.

Assessing Volitional Impairment

Since the *Hendricks* decision, case law has strongly supported the idea that the requisite mental disorder must somehow impair the individual's behavioral control (e.g., *In re Leon G.,* 2002; *In re Martinelli,* 2002; *In re Thorell,* 2003; *Kansas v. Crane,* 2002). However, the mental health field has yet to find an empirically supported method of distinguishing the irresistible impulse from the impulse simply not resisted. The legal community has long criticized mental health professionals for attributing control deficits to various diagnoses without a scientific base (Janus, 1998; La Fond, 2000; McAllister, 1998; Mercado et al., 2006; Mercado, Schopp, & Bornstein, 2005; Morse, 1998; Schopp et al., 1999; Winick, 1998). The preface to the *DSM-IV-TR* (2000) specifically cautions clinicians against assuming that any disorder implies a loss of control over one's behavior.

Research has identified a number of neuropsychological disorders that do affect behavioral control, most involving some form of orbitofrontal abnormality (Bechara, Damasio, & Damasio, 2000; Blair & Cipolitti, 2000; Burns & Swerdlow, 2003). However, many offenses committed by those deemed to be sexual predators are not the sudden, impulse-driven acts typically associated with brain dysfunction. Rather, they involve complex planning and often grooming (the gradual shaping of the child's behavior by the offender to gain the child's cooperation with sexual activity) of the target victims. Various authorities have argued that volitional impairment in sexual offenders is self-evident (Doren, 2002) and consistent with common sense (Hoberman, 1999). Others have suggested that relating a paraphilia to specific control deficits requires considerable inference, since there are no empirical data supporting the connection (Becker & Murphy, 1998).

BEWARE
Be careful
not to imply
a link between diagnosis
and volitional impairment
that has not been scientifically established.

Attorneys pursuing the commitment of individuals as SVPs often suggest that the case for volitional impairment be made from common sense. They would argue that because an individual fails to modify his behavior in the face of severe penalties or losses, that person must have substantial difficulty with behavioral control. However, forensic clinicians conducting FMHA in the SVP context are not asked to conduct assessments using only common sense. To date, the mental health professions have validated no method to determine whether an individual has more or less difficulty controlling behavior than the average person or the average sex offender. If such a method did exist, it would be even more challenging to link the control deficits to a particular diagnosis. This is especially true of the primary diagnoses used in SVP proceedings (i.e., paraphilias and personality disorders), given that the *DSM* defines these disorders in terms of behavioral descriptors rather than etiology (Lilienfeld, Waldman, & Israel, 1994; Miller et al., 2005). For example, there is no evidence to suggest that APD causes any difficulty in behavioral control, nor is there any method to measure the degree of difficulty or compare it to the control difficulties of the general offender population. Given this dearth of scientific data, evaluators are well advised to carefully select their language in describing disorders. Phrases such as "leads to . . . ," "results in . . . ," "manifests as . . . ," or "predisposes to . . . ," may imply a link between the diagnosis and future behavioral control that has not actually been established.

Measuring Risk

The most extensive research base for SVP evaluations lies in the area of risk assessment. Although precise base rates for sexual offending have not been established, extensive research in recent years has established solid static risk factors and provided intriguing evidence on some dynamic risk factors. Instruments have also been developed specifically to assess various types of risk.

The Issue of Base Rates

Risk assessments are often conducted by first establishing the overall base rate for the particular behavior and then comparing it to the particular offender's likelihood of engaging in the behavior. However, in the area of sexual offending, this has proven especially daunting, and very different conclusions have been reached by various researchers. In 1989, a review by Furby, Weinrott, and Blackshaw provided data suggesting base rates for reoffending ranging from 0% to 50%, depending in large part on the criterion applied. Using convictions as reoffending outcome, Hanson and Bussiere (1998) reported a recidivism average of 13.4% over 5 years. Bureau of Justice statistics from the 1990s suggested that sex offenders were no more likely to violate parole than other offenders (Heilbrun, Nezu, Keeney, Chung, and Wasserman, 1998). In a longitudinal study of reoffending in a sample of rapists, Prentky, Lee, Knight, and Cerce (1997) found that recidivism rose from 9% in the first year to 52% by the 25th year. Using charges as well as convictions as the criterion, Langevin and colleagues (2004) found that three in five offenders reoffended over 25 years; if other "undetected" offenses were considered, this figure rose to four out of five.

Part of the problem in establishing reasonable reoffending base rates involves the tendency noted earlier to treat sex offenders as a homogeneous group, or, at most, separating rapists from child molesters. Researchers (e.g., Doren & Epperson, 2001; Furby et al., 1989; Hanson & Bussiere, 1998; Rice & Harris, 1997) have indicated significant differences between various groups of offenders. The outcome used also affects the base rate that is reported. Very different results may be observed using convictions only, as opposed to charges, allegations, or self-report. The "convictions only" outcome, although the most specific (accurately identifying the cases in which sexual reoffending did not occur), is also the least sensitive (missing the most cases in which sexual reoffending did take place) (Abel et al., 1987; Barbaree & Marshall, 1988; Doren, 1998). Finally, offenses measured by rearrest may be revised through plea bargaining and classifying by the most serious offense, such as homicide (Quinsey, Harris, Rice, & Cormier, 2006).

BEWARE
Reliable base rates are difficult to establish. Note limits on their accuracy when using them.

Given these significant problems with base rates, evaluators are advised to consider them with caution and provide caveats as to their limitations. Prentky and Burgess (2000) appropriately summarized this issue: "Perhaps the simplest summary is that consideration of base rate data is indeed critical to accurate decision-making, but that (1) the unreliability of such data on sex offenders compromises their usefulness and (2) the overarching goal of community safety may place a higher premium on inaccuracy" (p. 113). In other words, using community safety as the primary objective would mean that a false negative prediction would be of much greater concern than a false positive. An evaluator should consider which study or studies provide the most useful data for estimating the base rate of sexual reoffending in the relevant population during the relevant time frame, and the evaluator should be prepared to discuss that on direct- or cross-examination. In any case, a decision on how heavily to tilt an SVP commitment decision toward either false positives or false negatives is beyond the purview of the evaluator, as it is squarely in the domains of courts and policy makers. The evaluator should strive for accuracy and describe clearly any limitations on the accuracy of her opinion.

Risk Factors

Over the past three decades, research data have grown exponentially regarding risk factors for general violence and for sexual reoffending. Research has been replicated in a variety of settings and with a variety of subjects to provide the evaluator with several key factors that appear very solid. For the most part, these risk factors have been static—that is, not changeable in response to planned intervention.

HISTORY

One factor repeatedly found to indicate high risk for reoffending is past history of sexual offending (Hanson & Bussiere, 1998; Prentky, Knight, & Lee, 1997; Quinsey, 1986; Rice,

INFO

Factors related to risk of reoffending include the following:

- History of sexual offending
- Deviant interests
- Psychopathy
- Younger age of offender
- Violating conditions of treatment or release
- Offending against males or strangers
- Never been married or in a committed relationship

Harris, & Quinsey, 1990). Some investigators have made the argument that the targeted outcome should not be limited to sexual offenses. Quinsey et al. (2006) point out that general violent offending is more likely to capture serious sexual offenses that are not so labeled (e.g., homicides). Although presenting data to support their argument, they also suggest examining an individual's pattern of offenses, since chronic sexual offenders tend to repeat similar crimes.

DEVIANCE

Having deviant interests is a second factor that is very strongly connected to sexual recidivism (Hanson & Bussiere, 1998; Harris et al., 2003; Proulx et al., 1997; Rice et al., 1990). Campbell (2004) has quite reasonably criticized this factor as being poorly defined. It is generally described in behavioral terms as abusing small children or humiliating or torturing one's victims. It has often been measured in research settings using the penile plethysmograph. Multiple studies have found the plethysmograph able to distinguish deviant from nondeviant sexual preferences (Harris, Rice, Quinsey, Chaplin, & Earls, 1992; Harris & Rice, 1996; Lalumiere & Harris, 1998; Lalumiere & Quinsey, 1994; Hall, Shondrick, & Hirschman, 1993). However, the plethysmograph has also been criticized for the lack of uniformity in its administration and in training for plethysmographers, the various ways in which data are interpreted, the absence of norms for subgroups of sexual offenders, and its susceptibility to faking (Marshall & Fernandez, 2000; Miller et al., 2005; Prentky & Burgess, 2000, Wilson, 1998). Other studies indicate that the instrument is much less useful with rapists than with child molesters (Hanson & Bussiere, 1998; Marshall & Fernandez, 2000). Nor is it particularly useful with individuals who have completed treatment (Quinsey et al., 2006).

PSYCHOPATHY

During the discussion of diagnoses, psychopathy was mentioned as a potential risk factor for sexual recidivism. It has been demonstrated to be more strongly predictive of general recidivism than of sexual recidivism (Quinsey, Rice, and Harris; 1995). It is also much more predictive of risk in rapists than in child molesters, because many fewer child molesters score in the psychopathic range (Hare, 2003;

Porter et al., 2000; Rice & Harris, 1997). It is important to reiterate that although a high score on the PCL-R may be associated with higher risk, a low score cannot necessarily be translated into low risk. Rather, the low score would mean that there is one risk factor that the individual does not have. Child molesters who have no other criminal record are unlikely to have an elevated PCL-R score even if they have molested multiple victims (Bauer, 2006; Porter et al., 2000). This result is probably due to the PCL-R scoring process, which measures traits that recur across a variety of situations and contexts. However, should the individual being evaluated both score high on the PCL-R *and* have multiple victims, the person is apt to be at very high risk for recidivism (Hildebrand, de Ruiter, & Vogel, 2004; Rice & Harris, 1997; Serin et al., 2001).

YOUNGER AGE
Age has been found to be negatively related to risk for sexual reoffending. The highest rate for recidivism appears to be found in males of ages 18–30, with the recidivism rate for those released after age 60 being less than 5% (Hanson, 2002). However, this trend was less true for child molesters, whose rate of reoffense declined more slowly with age. A second way in which age is related to risk concerns the age at first sexual offense. The younger the individual when the first offense was committed, the more likely the person is to recidivate (Hanson & Bussiere, 1998; Quinsey et al., 2006).

VIOLATING CONDITIONS
People who fail to cooperate with treatment or otherwise violate conditions of release have been found to be at higher risk (Epperson, Kaul, & Hasselton, 1998; Hanson, 1998; Hanson & Bussiere, 1998; Hanson & Harris, 1998). However, this should not be interpreted as proving the effectiveness of any treatment or condition; rather, it is the willingness to abide by established rules that appears to be critical. Risk is apparently related simply to the failure to follow prescribed conditions rather than to what the specific conditions may be. This is exemplified by Hanson and Bussiere's (1998) finding that failure to complete treatment was a significant correlate of recidivism—regardless of the nature of the treatment.

BEWARE
Static risk factors do not reflect how an individual may change, for example, in response to treatment or after incarceration.

Items related to supervision failure are included on several of the actuarial instruments and structured guides (e.g., Violence Risk Appraisal Guide [VRAG], Historical, Clinical, Risk management–20 [HCR-20], Minnesota Sex Offender Screening Tool, Revised [MnSOST-R]) without any cause for the failure being specified.

OTHER RELATED FACTORS

Several other factors have consistently demonstrated some relationship with future risk. Those who offend against males, as well as those who perpetrate against strangers, are generally at higher risk for reoffending (Hanson & Bussiere, 1998; Proulx et al., 1997) than those who offend against females or known victims. In addition, persons who have never been married or otherwise involved in a committed relationship with an adult partner pose a greater risk (Hanson & Bussiere, 1998).

Static Risk Factors

Static risk factors have been the strongest predictors identified for use in actuarial risk tools. However, they also have limitations that should not be overlooked. They are acontextual—that is, they do not take into consideration the individual's future situation or context. They are also unaffected by both time and intervention, considered beginning at present and going forward. If evaluations were based only on static indicators, then evaluations would not reflect how any individual changed. Static indicators can be very valuable at the time of initial evaluation. However, they are not helpful as an indicator of treatment response or change following a term of incarceration.

Dynamic Risk Factors

More recently, some research has attempted to investigate risk factors that have the potential to change over time or through planned intervention—particularly those that might be targeted by intervention programs. Although results are still

INFO
Empirically supported dynamic risk factors can be critical if the objective of the evaluation is release planning or ongoing risk management.

preliminary, several factors have been identified that merit further study. These include poor social supports, an emotional preoccupation with children, attitudes tolerant of sexual assault, antisocial lifestyles, hostility, poor self-management strategies, substance abuse, poor cooperation with supervision, employment instability, and sexual preoccupations (Hanson & Harris, 2000; Hanson & Morton-Bourgon, 2004, 2005). Dynamic factors can be either relatively stable or acute. For example, an individual may have a general problem with substance abuse that can be treated (stable) or she may be intoxicated at the moment (acute).

Illusory Correlations

In addition to investigating factors that have been found to be predictive of risk, it is also essential that evaluators avoid using those that are unrelated to risk. Intuition and conventional wisdom can muddy the risk assessment waters. Clinicians often mistakenly assume that taking responsibility for the offense, demonstrating empathy for the victim, verbalizing motivation for change, and successfully completing treatment equate to lower risk; however, well-controlled research has failed to demonstrate these relationships (Hanson & Bussiere, 1998; Hanson & Morton-Bourgon, 2004, 2005; Marques, Wiederanders, Day, Nelson, & van Ommeren, 2005). Successfully reaching goals outlined in treatment programs has also failed to predict a reduction in recidivism (Barbaree & Marshall, 1998; Quinsey, Khanna, & Malcolm, 1998; Rice, Harris, & Quinsey, 1991; Seto & Barbaree, 1999). Finally, there is a commonly held belief that being the victim of childhood abuse indicates a high propensity to commit repeated sexual offenses; research has not supported this view (Hanson & Bussiere, 1998; Hanson & Morton-Bourgon, 2004, 2005).

BEWARE
The following factors do NOT predict reduced risk:

- Taking responsibility for the offense
- Demonstrating empathy for the victim
- Verbalizing motivation
- Successfully completing treatment objectives

Instruments

Traditional psychological tests (e.g., personality inventories, intelligence tests, achievement batteries) are often of little help in conducting an assessment in the context of SVP commitment.

The PCL-R, however, although not designed as a risk assessment instrument, has been very helpful because of the strong correlation between psychopathy and various types of recidivism. Beyond that, over the past two decades a number of instruments have been developed specifically to assist clinicians in systemizing the assessment of sexual offenders. These can be roughly categorized into actuarial assessment instruments and structured guides.

ACTUARIAL INSTRUMENTS

The true actuarial instrument is a set of specific elements that can be assigned a numerical weighting based upon clearly operationalized criteria that can then be entered into a carefully weighted formula that generates a risk score or category. Actuarial instruments commonly used in SVP evaluations are listed in Table 3.1.

There are those who argue persuasively that the actuarial approach is always superior to any clinical assessment and should replace clinical judgment of any kind (Grove & Meehl, 1996; Quinsey et al., 2006). The predictive validity of such instruments can be established scientifically and

Table 3.1 | Actuarial Instruments Frequently Used in Forensic Evaluation of SVP Candidates

Instrument	Source
Minnesota Sex Offender Screening Tool–Revised (MnSOST-R)	Epperson, Kaul, & Hesselton, 1998
Rapid Risk Assessment for Sex Offender Recidivism (RRASOR)	Hanson, 1997
Sex Offender Risk Appraisal Guide (SORAG)	Quinsey et al., 1998, 2006
*Static-99	Hanson & Thornton, 1999
Violence Risk Appraisal Guide (VRAG)	Quinsey et al., 1998, 2006

*The Static-2002 was in the final research process at the time of this writing.

BEWARE
Limitations of
actuarial
instruments include the
following:

- Inconsistent results of predictive validity studies

- Lack of consideration of context

- No measurement of dynamic factors and change

replicated across a variety of populations. Much of the information required for most actuarial instruments can be obtained and verified from records and collateral interviews, reducing the concern over the veracity of self-report. A number of the instruments include very specific instructions that virtually eliminate the need for clinical judgment, so the instruments can be completed by non-clinicians. Most instruments have been published and widely peer reviewed—a factor that can be helpful in the face of a *Frye* or *Daubert* challenge.

However, before deciding the extent to which actuarial instruments should be incorporated into an evaluation, clinicians should be aware of several disadvantages of these tools. To date, studies comparing the predictive validity of the various actuarial instruments have yielded inconsistent results (Barbaree et al., 2001; Bartosh, Garby, Lewis, & Gray, 2003; de Vogel, de Ruiter, van Beek & Mead, 2004; Rice & Harris, 1997; Stadtland, Hollweg, Dietl, Reich, & Nedopil, 2005). If one were to follow the advice of Quinsey et al. (2006) and use only the results of the actuarial assessment to predict future violent or sexual offending behavior, then the influence of context would not be considered. In addition, these instruments often place many more subjects in the high-risk category than the relatively small number that state systems typically wish to commit. For the process of forensic mental health assessment, the evaluator typically reviews extensive records and conducts collateral interviews in the attempt to ensure that results from nomothetic measures apply well to this individual. Finally, as these methods rely heavily on static variables, they are not useful in measuring change. Therefore, there is the assumption that risk is not subject to change, which is problematic if, in a given case, one is attempting to assess a change in risk over time. One actuarial instrument aimed at measuring dynamic factors, the Sex Offender Needs Assessment Rating (SONAR), is currently under development (Hanson & Harris, 2000).

3
chapter

STRUCTURED GUIDES

An alternative to the strict actuarial approach is the *structured clinical guide*. These instruments contain a number of variables that have an empirical relationship to risk for the clinician to apply to the individual being evaluated. Although some scoring may be suggested, no specific numerical result translates to a level of risk. In fact, proponents of this approach insist that in clinical assessment of this kind, "it makes little sense to sum the number of risk factors present in a given case, and then use fixed, arbitrary cutoffs to classify the individual as low, moderate, or high risk. . . . It is both possible and reasonable for an assessor to conclude that an assessee is at high risk for violence based on the presence of a single factor" (Webster, Douglas, Eaves, & Hart, 1997, p. 22). Structured guides commonly used in SVP evaluations are listed in Table 3.2.

Structured guides have the advantage of being peer reviewed and published. They are particularly helpful in reducing bias and ensuring that no important issue is overlooked. Dynamic and static factors are considered.

Structured guides also have certain disadvantages. Although each element is backed by research, there are factors included that also have negative results in the literature. For example, the SVR-20 includes the factor "victim of child abuse"; however, a number of research studies did not find this to be related to recidivism (Hanson & Bussiere, 1998; Hanson & Morton-Bourgon, 2004, 2005). Structured professional judgment (SPJ) guides depend on accurate professional judgment being

BEWARE
Unrelated factors and poor clinical judgment may yield inaccurate results when using structured guides.

Table 3.2 | Structured Professional Judgment Guides Frequently Used in Forensic Evaluation of SVP Candidates

Instrument	Source
Historical/Clinical/Risk Management Scheme (HCR-20)	Webster et al., 1997
Sexual Violence Risk–20 (SVR-20)	Boer, Hart, Kropp, & Webster, 1997

exercised, and cannot be completed by non-clinicians. The amount of weight to assign to any one element is left completely to clinical judgment; when such judgment is inaccurate, the results yielded by the tool are likewise less accurate than would otherwise be the case.

Risk Management Techniques

Depending on the jurisdiction, evaluators may be asked for recommendations on reducing risk. This would be particularly important if the issue at hand involves discharge from commitment.

Medication

Chemical intervention is one of the two primary clinical treatments used with sex offenders. When medication is used for this purpose, it is generally a progestronal hormone compound, such as medroxy-progesterone (MPA). Although some evidence has emerged suggesting that this may reduce recidivism in child molesters (Harris et al., 1998), a major meta-analysis failed to support this finding (Gallagher, Wilson, Hirschfield, Coggeshall, & MacKenzie, 1999).

Compliance has been found to be a major drawback to this treatment, as side effects can be particularly distressing (Kravitz et al., 1995; Miller, 1998; Stalans, 2004). Additionally, there is no convincing evidence that the majority of sexual offenders have heightened sex drives (Rosler & Witztum, 2000).

Psychotherapy

The second commonly used clinical intervention is psychotherapy, often provided in a very structured program setting. Research on therapy programs remains extremely mixed. There appears to be a general consensus that traditional psychodynamic, insight-oriented approaches have not been effective, and these have given way to cognitive behavioral treatment (Conroy, 2003). Initial research suggested moderate, but positive, outcomes (Hall, 1995; Hildebran & Pithers, 1992). However, much of the early research has been questioned because of methodological

INFO

The primary clinical treatments include the following:

- Medication
- Psychotherapy

However, evidence of their ability to reduce recidivism is mixed.

flaws (Marshall & Anderson, 1996; McConaghy, 1999), including a lack of adequate controls, selective sampling, and poor outcome criteria. Since then, research findings have often been contradictory, with some studies showing positive effects (Hanson et al., 2002) and others yielding little or no effect (Hanson, Broom, & Stephenson, 2004). One of the most anticipated and well-controlled studies, conducted at Atascadero State Hospital, yielded no differences in recidivism between the treated and untreated groups after 8 years (Marques et al., 2005). An examination of the empirical literature to date would yield the same conclusion reached by Prentky and Burgess (2000): "At the present time, the most informed and dispassionate conclusion must be that we simply do not know what percentage of the aggregated (highly heterogeneous) population of sex offenders can return to a nonoffending lifestyle through treatment" (p. 217). This is not to say that treatment is never effective or that efforts to treat sexual offenders should be abandoned. However, it is important that evaluators be honest with the courts regarding what is known about treatment outcome.

Nonclinical Interventions

Some programs designed to reduce sex offender recidivism go well beyond traditional clinical treatment. Known broadly as the "containment approach," these programs attempt to implement every conceivable intervention with the primary goal of ensuring public safety. These may include (but are not limited to) geographic restrictions, required polygraphs and plethysmographs, specially trained probation officers, electronic monitoring, Internet restrictions, and various forms of counseling (although treatment is only a secondary goal). These plans almost universally include a waiver of confidentiality so that all information is shared with the entire criminal justice team (McGrath, Cumming, & Holt, 2002; Meyer, Molett, Richards, Arnold, & Latham, 2003).

Some data, independent of the broader model, are available regarding the plethysmograph and polygraph as treatment tools, both of which are recommended by the ATSA (1993). Technical problems with the former were discussed earlier in this chapter. The reliability of polygraph results remains a topic of debate (Branaman &

BEWARE
Containment programs
use a number of different methods at once, making their efficacy difficult to assess.

Gallagher, 2005; Oksol & O'Donohue, 2004). In a very favorable review, the results of the polygraph with sex offenders were concluded to be 85% accurate (Grubin & Madsen, 2006). Of course, this means that results were inaccurate 15% of the time. This is of greatest concern when stakes are high. Particular concern has been raised over the lack of consistent standards for polygraph examiners (Grubin & Madsen, 2005). Beyond the issue of accuracy, however, is that of overall utility. Both the plethysmograph and the polygraph are seen by their supporters as tools to break down denial (Association for the Treatment of Sexual Abusers, 1993; Dutton & Emerick, 1996). Yet sizable research studies have found the correlation between denial and recidivism to be close to zero (Hanson & Bussiere, 1998; Hanson & Morton-Bourgon, 2004).

Containment programs as a whole must be considered very carefully, as they are clearly very resource intensive for providers and may be extremely burdensome for the offenders. Not surprisingly, a survey of probation officers who used the approach found that they perceived it to be very effective (English, Pullen, & Jones, 1996). One program evaluation study, involving a 2-year follow-up of three Illinois programs, found mildly positive outcome results; however, many of the subjects were described as "hands-off offenders" (those who do not touch their victims) (Stalans, 2004). The very complexity of the approach makes it extremely difficult to assess adequately. If positive results are obtained, which of the myriad of interventions are actually responsible? Does each add incremental validity? Do some, in fact, inhibit the positive outcome? Additionally, no two programs appear to use the exact same protocol. Therefore, at the present time, no definitive conclusions about the effectiveness of the containment approach can be drawn from the empirical literature.

Assessment Practice

Courts frequently seek information on the general practice in a particular type of assessment. In states that rely on the *Frye* test in determining what is admissible as expert evidence, "general acceptance in

BEWARE Common use of an assessment method in the field does not establish validity or reliability itself.

the particular field" (*Frye v. United States*, 1923) is the single test. In states that look to *Daubert*, it is one of four suggested criteria (*Daubert v. Merrell Dow Pharmaceuticals*, 1993). The other three *Daubert* criteria are as follows: the theory or technique must be falsifiable, refutable, and testable; it must have been subjected to peer review and publication; and it must have a known error rate. Therefore, it is informative for evaluators to see how others in the field analyze relevant issues. However, it is important to note that having a large number of practitioners use a given assessment method is not necessarily evidence of the method's validity or reliability.

Texas Study

One study, completed in Texas, analyzed the contents of 104 SVP evaluations conducted by 19 evaluators over a 5-year period (Amenta, 2005). Data on a large number of variables are reported. Of particular interest is the consideration of diagnoses, the use of actuarial measures, the attention to volition, the inclusion of psychopathy, the reliance on risk factors, and the conclusion regarding the ultimate legal issue. Of the total reports, 98% included an Axis I and/or Axis II diagnosis. The single most common diagnosis was antisocial personality disorder, followed by substance-related disorders, and then pedophilia; only 6% of reports used paraphilia NOS. Less than a fourth used results from the Static-99 or MnSOST-R tests. However, this may be because these two instruments are generally the basis for screening inmates for an SVP evaluation in Texas, and almost all those referred were already known to have high scores. Only 16 reports (15%) addressed the issue of volition. Psychopathy, which is a required part of SVP assessment in Texas, was addressed in 91% of all reports and was always evaluated using the PCL-R. The most common risk factor cited as important was the individual's history of sexual offending. However, there was considerable variability in whether evaluators considered prior offenses as reflected in official reports on convictions or charges, or self-reported prior offenses, or some combination of the two. In addition, evaluators often failed to identify risk factors substantiated by the literature, while using factors not empirically established as predictive of reoffending (e.g., denial). Finally, it is interesting to note than only 21% of reports included an ultimate issue opinion (the individual should be committed as an SVP), and only 44% contained an opinion on the penultimate issue (the person suffers from a behavioral abnormality that makes it likely that he would engage in predatory acts of sexual violence after release). An intriguing finding was that neither diagnosis nor identified risk factors in the reports appeared to be related to the prosecutor's decision to actually file for SVP commitment.

Florida Study

The Florida study (Levensen & Morin, 2006) cannot be compared directly to the Texas study, as the research method was quite different. Levensen and Morin mainly examined the relationship between data used and commitment recommendations made by evaluators (apparently the ultimate issue was typically addressed). Of the 448 reports, the most common diagnosis was a substance-related disorder. This was followed by antisocial personality disorder and pedophilia, with paraphilia NOS cited in 30% of cases. However, only pedophilia and paraphilia NOS were highly correlated with recommendations for commitment. Strong correlations were found between commitment recommendations and actuarial instrument scores, which suggests that these were heavily used. Although psychopathy was related to ultimate issue opinions, a significant number of evaluators did not use the PCL-R. Enough data are available to indicate that evaluators in these two states took somewhat different approaches.

Test Survey

Archer, Buffington-Vollum, Stredny, and Handel (2006) surveyed members of the American Psychology–Law Society (Division 41 of the APA) and the American Academy of Forensic Psychology (forensic psychology diplomates of the American Board of Professional Psychology) to gauge patterns of psychological test usage common in forensic evaluations. Of the 97 respondents who conducted general risk assessments, over 50% reported never, rarely, or only occasionally using the PCL-R, the HCR-20, the VRAG, or the Level of Service Inventory–Revised (LSI-R), with the modal response for all but the PCL-R being "never."

Of the 62 respondents who conducted sex offender risk assessments, over 50% endorsed "never," "rarely," or "only occasionally" using the Static 99, SVR-20, MnSOST-R, RRASOR, or SORAG, with the modal response for each instrument again being "never." Based on these numbers, it would be difficult to contend that the administration of specially designed risk assessment instruments represents the approach used by the majority of practitioners in the field.

Conclusions

A meaningful understanding of the SVP population is limited because of the frequent treatment of sex offenders in the literature as a homogenous group or, at best, subdivided only by age of the victim. Scientific assessment methods are limited for the task of establishing the requisite disorder for SVP commitments and virtually nonexistent for addressing volitional impairment. However, considerable research is available to assist the evaluator in assessing risk for this population, including both identified risk factors and validated instruments. The body of literature is quickly expanding, although there is little consistency in how the information is used in practice.

APPLICATION

Preparation for the Evaluation | 4

Before beginning the process of actually evaluating an individual for possible commitment as a sexually violent predator, the forensic clinician should construct a plan of action and assemble appropriate materials. This will involve gaining a clear understanding of the nature of the work for which one is appointed and the rules of the particular jurisdiction in which the evaluation is to be done. Evaluators should also assess the types of collateral information to be gathered and assemble this information. Finally, evaluators will want to carefully anticipate questions and ethical quandaries that may arise and be prepared to address them.

Types of Evaluation Appointments

Forensic mental health assessments typically occur at a number of critical junctures in the process of SVP civil commitments. The initial phase generally encompasses a triage process in which some agency or authority considers all of the potential offenders having sexual offense histories compatible with statutory requirements. The agency or authority recommends which of these individuals should be evaluated for commitment. Once recommendations are completed, it is generally prosecutors (or attorneys representing the state) who make final decisions regarding petitions to be filed. Following a filing with the court, the judge may appoint an additional expert or experts of its own, and both defense and prosecution typically retain mental health professionals, depending on the jurisdiction.

The Initial Triage Stage

Many jurisdictions use employees of the agency having custody of the individual to conduct the evaluation. Typically this would be the Department of Corrections, the Department of Health (or Mental

INFO

State statutes on conducting assessments vary greatly. For example, South Carolina simply refers to a review of records. By contrast, California and Texas both have specific protocols that must be followed. Florida requires that the protocol include at least the offer of an interview, although not necessarily at the initial screening stage. North Dakota and Virginia suggest, but do not mandate, the use of actuarial as well as clinical methods.

Health), or a designated hospital facility. The skills and qualifications of these evaluators are often left to the discretion of the agency. Some statutes provide little guidance on how these assessments are to be conducted.

Some jurisdictions typically eliminate a large number of potential offenders from the pool at this stage, whereas others do not. During the first 6 months following passage of the Jimmy Ryce Act, Florida referred over 2,600 individuals to attorneys for the state, a number suggesting that few potential eligibles were eliminated (LaFond, 2005). Texas, by contrast, generally releases over 900 sexual offenders annually, but selects fewer than 300 for possible commitment at this initial phase (Texas Department of Criminal Justice, 2002).

Multidisciplinary Teams

Once initial data are gathered by the appointed agency, they are often submitted to a multidisciplinary team (as occurs in Florida, Missouri, South Carolina, and Texas, for instance) or end-of-sentence referral subcommittee (e.g., Washington) for further analysis and triage. Members of this group are generally appointed by the agency and have varying levels of expertise. Some states require that most members be mental health professionals; others have no such requirement or very limited mental health representation. For example, South Carolina has a five-member team; only one member must be a trained, qualified clinician with expertise in working with sex offenders. Some states (e.g., Texas) require that the team contract with an outside expert or experts for additional evaluation. In jurisdictions where this is not the case, those charged with the initial data gathering become even more critical to the process.

BEWARE
If offenders are not placed in the highest risk category at triage stage, it may trigger their release without any judicial process involved, given that these individuals will not be referred for further judicial review.

Community Notification and Registration

If individual sex offenders are not among those selected for referral to the prosecution unit, these initial evaluations may still have a significant impact on their lives. Although all jurisdictions now have community registration laws, many also have community notification requirements that may not apply to all registered offenders. In addition to the registration requirement, notification mandates law enforcement agencies to make the registration information available to community members. This is a regulation that many offenders find onerous and intrusive. Some jurisdictions use what LaFond calls the "Active Agency-Conducted Notification Based on Individualized Risk Determination" (2005, p. 89) model. These jurisdictions, such as Washington, often rely on the releasing agency to determine whether an offender should be subject to community notification.

The Outside Expert

States have various ways of selecting outside experts for appointment to SVP proceedings. In some cases a designated agency may simply contract with private practitioners, often on a competitive-bid basis. The court can also appoint its own expert. Some jurisdictions maintain lists of available and qualified mental health professionals, but these lists are not binding on the court. Typically, once a petition for commitment has been filed, both defense and prosecution teams will hire additional experts. Most statutes require that the court appoint and fund an expert for an indigent respondent; however, this may not be the expert of his choice. Anecdotal evidence suggests that there is often a limited pool of mental health professionals who are qualified for and interested in performing this type of evaluation. Therefore, it is not unusual for a small group of professionals to testify in a large percentage of the cases in a given jurisdiction.

4
chapter

Reexamination of Those Committed

Every SVP commitment law provides that those who are committed will be periodically reexamined. This is to determine whether they continue to have the disorder that makes them likely to commit additional sexual violence if released and whether the danger that they

INFO

Even those evaluations that do not lead to referral for SVP commitment may subject an offender to community registration and notification.

BEWARE
An individual's treating clinician should not act as his evaluator.

present to society is still sufficient to require confinement. These follow-up evaluations generally occur annually unless a special petition is filed. About half of these evaluations are conducted by personnel at the facility in which the person is held (Doren, 2002). An important consideration in these instances is that the evaluation be conducted by someone other than the individual's treating clinician. The most common other arrangement involves having a mental health professional either appointed by the court or hired by an attorney. One state, New Jersey, uses a team of evaluation psychologists who, like the treating psychologists, are employed by the civil-commitment facility.

Texas has a very different procedure. Since SVP commitment in Texas can be outpatient only, there is no facility readily available to provide reassessment. Once the individual has been committed, treatment is under the purview of the Council for Sex Offender Treatment (CSOT)—an entity that is also authorized by statute to issue a special license to anyone providing treatment to these offenders. Only a small minority of those holding this license are doctoral-level mental health professionals; many have masters degrees in some discipline but often lack training and experience in treatment and assessment beyond how to provide a specific type of cognitive behavioral therapy (CBT) to sex offenders. The CSOT selects someone holding such a special license to conduct the reevaluation. The individual assigned is often the treatment provider, creating substantial problems with dual roles in a single case.

Rules Specific to the Jurisdiction

This section provides numerous examples of how various jurisdictions configure the procedures for SVP evaluations.

Expert Qualifications

Most jurisdictions leave it to the agency involved to formulate rules on who conducts the initial pre-commitment evaluations and who is eligible to serve on multidisciplinary teams. Most, but not all, jurisdictions refer to a psychologist or psychiatrist to perform the

BEST PRACTICE
Be familiar with laws and practices in the relevant jurisdiction, and never assume that policies are necessarily similar in other jurisdictions.

evaluation. For example, Missouri's law defines a mental health professional as a psychiatrist, psychiatric resident, psychologist, psychiatric nurse, or psychiatric social worker. Massachusetts mandates at least 2 years of experience in working with sex offenders. A number of states (e.g., Illinois, Massachusetts, New Jersey, Texas) require that a psychiatrist be involved in the process. This is often due to other laws mandating medical evaluation in civil commitment cases. Texas law, for instance, indicates that no one can be civilly committed without competent medical testimony. Given the often vague qualifications specified by SVP statutes, it may fall to mental health professionals to determine whether to proffer themselves as experts in this type of assessment. In considering the appropriateness of one's knowledge, skill, training, and experience to assist the court in this type of decision-making, it is important to consider both clinical and forensic areas.

CLINICAL EXPERTISE

In the clinical arena, it is relatively rare for a sex offender to have a major psychotic disorder. In fact, Florida now specifically excludes from SVP commitment those persons whose sexual offenses were caused solely by psychosis. Rather, diagnoses of personality disorder and/or a paraphilia are most common.

BEST PRACTICE
When judging your expert qualifications, be sure to consider your familiarity in the following areas:

Clinical

- Assessment tools
- Research on risk assessment and risk management
- Research on treatment effectiveness

Forensic

- Statutes, case law, and rules governing jurisdiction of practice
- Rights of evaluees
- Guidelines for ethical practice
- Commonly encountered dilemmas

Evaluation often involves some type of testing. A number of specialized forensic assessment instruments have become available in recent years to evaluate both risk for general recidivism (encompassing *all* reoffending) and risk for sexual recidivism. Evaluators must be familiar with available specialty tools and understand their important psychometric properties. We recommend that evaluators be familiar with the commonly used tools even if they do not plan to use a specific tool, so they can explain why the tool was (or was not) used.

It is also crucial that evaluators be familiar with current research relating to risk assessment and risk management, a literature that has grown exponentially in recent years. The construct of psychopathy—another area of burgeoning research—is important in some sex offender evaluations. As a population, sex offenders are both heterogeneous and unique; thus experience in working with sex offenders is critical. Evaluators must be familiar with the research on treatment effectiveness to make reasonable prognoses and risk management recommendations, regardless of whether the evaluator is an active treatment provider.

FORENSIC EXPERTISE

In the forensic arena, it is vital to understand the statutes, case law, and rules governing the jurisdiction of practice. Anyone conducting these assessments must be aware of the rights of evaluees, as applicable in one's jurisdiction. For example, is the individual required to cooperate in all interviews? Must the individual be competent for SVP proceedings? Is the individual entitled to counsel at this phase of the evaluation? Beyond laws, guidelines for ethical practice (e.g., the *Ethical Principles of Psychologists and Code of Conduct* [American Psychological Association, 2002]; *Specialty Guidelines for Forensic Psychologists* [Committee on Ethical Guidelines for Forensic Psychologists, 1991], and *Ethical Guidelines for the Practice of Forensic Psychiatry* [American Academy of Psychiatry and the Law, 2005]) and commonly encountered dilemmas need to be understood. Finally, it is one thing to know and understand relevant data and procedures; it is another to be able to communicate these effectively to lawyers, judges, and juries.

TRIER OF FACT

Of course, it is ultimately the province of the trier of fact to determine who will be credentialed as an expert to provide evaluations and testimony. Beyond those providing assessments of an individual respondent, this will also apply to those serving as experts on the "state of the science," whose role may involve describing and explaining relevant data about risk or diagnoses or procedures, but not with regard to the specific individual. The professional's role in this process is to provide an accurate, complete explanation of one's background, experience, and abilities.

Time Frames

Most SVP statutes include time frames governing every stage of these evaluations. In Florida, for example, in the normal course of events, SVP consideration can begin as much as 18 months prior to potential release from incarceration, allowing more than sufficient time. However, Florida also has a provision to deal with unexpected events, such as a judge finding that the individual's original sentence was illegal or improper and that the individual should thus be immediately released. Under those circumstances, the SVP program can hold the individual for 72 hours, at the end of which the state attorney must file a petition or the person must be released. In those special cases, the evaluation must be conducted within the 72 hours and the evaluator must prepare a written summary of her findings. It is important that evaluators be attentive to the time allotted for evaluations in the jurisdiction, as violations could result in a case not being allowed to proceed. Some time frames are by statute; others are by agency rules or contract. However, in reality, such time constraints rarely keep courts from finding a way to hold proceedings in which public safety is at issue—for example, by adjourning a commitment hearing to a later date. Nonetheless, careful attention to time limits can significantly reduce problems and enhance one's credibility.

BEST PRACTICE

Pay careful attention to time frames governing each stage of evaluation as specified by state statutes or agency policies.

4
chapter

Right to Counsel

The right to representation by legal counsel during proceedings in which liberty interests are at stake is very important in our society. The U.S. Supreme Court clearly established this right for both those accused in criminal court (*Argersinger v. Hamlin,* 1972) and juveniles (*In re Gault,* 1967). Psychologists have supported this in the *Specialty Guidelines for Forensic Psychologists:*

> VI.D. Forensic psychologists do not provide professional forensic services to a defendant or to any party in, or in contemplation of, a legal proceeding prior to that individual's representation by counsel, except for persons judicially determined, where appropriate, to be handling their representation *pro se.* When the forensic services are pursuant to court order and the client is not represented by

counsel, the forensic psychologist makes reasonable efforts to inform the court prior to providing services. (Committee for Ethical Guidelines for Forensic Psychologists, 1991, p. 661)

Nonetheless, the legal requirement for representation by counsel is less clearly defined in the arena of civil commitment. All jurisdictions having SVP laws provide the right to counsel and appointed counsel for the indigent in SVP proceedings. However, this generally does not apply until a commitment petition has been filed with the court. For example, the North Dakota statute is very specific that counsel must be provided within 24 hours of the filing. However, certain kinds of evaluations in SVP cases—those that help determine which offenders will be considered for commitment proceedings—are conducted before the petition is filed. Evaluations are assembled by interdisciplinary teams and forwarded to the prosecution before any filing. Yet evaluations done during this period are typically maintained in the file, can be entered into evidence in a commitment hearing, and may be supplemented by evaluator testimony during the hearing. Thus the offender may be without legal advice prior to the initial evaluation, and may even be unaware that an evaluation is to be done until the forensic clinician arrives.

The right to counsel throughout the relevant procedures was raised in court by a Texas inmate in 2002. The court ruled that, absent a petition for commitment, no such right applied—and the court had no obligation at this stage to provide funding for attorneys representing the indigent (*Beasley v. Molett*, 2002). A notice was then forwarded to all evaluators by the Texas Department of Criminal Justice instructing them not to give offenders incorrect information regarding right to counsel. This was important information for evaluators, albeit surprising to a number of them.

CASE LAW

Beasley v. Molett,
2002

● The Texas Ninth District Court of Appeals ruled that no right to counsel applied at the evaluation stage prior to the filing of a petition for commitment.

STRATEGIES

To alleviate potential ethical concerns that might arise in such situations, several strategies might be helpful:

• Evaluators might negotiate with the department having custody of the offenders to provide information for inmates regarding the law, its potential consequences, and any relevant legal rights prior to any formal evaluation. This approach has proved somewhat effective in Texas. Following complaints from forensic clinicians, the Texas Department of Criminal Justice instituted some formal psycholegal information sessions for offenders prior to evaluations taking place.

- Evaluators might approach the interview prepared to provide information regarding free or inexpensive legal services that might be available.

- Evaluators might approach any legal service that generally handles cases of those incarcerated and encourage its staff to provide information and/or a forum to raise questions for those potentially subject to civil commitment.

- If an offender is surprised by a request for evaluation, the evaluator could agree to reschedule the appointment until the person has had an opportunity to consult with his attorney.

- The evaluator could make specific arrangements to ensure that the evaluee is informed about the evaluation prior to the appointment time.

One strategy to avoid, however, is providing anything that might be construed as legal advice. There may be a fine line between informing individuals of their legal rights (an ethically appropriate act) and advising them how to exercise these rights. A common question from individuals who have not had the advice of counsel is, "Will it help me if I answer all of your questions and take your tests?" Evaluating forensic clinicians are rarely trained as attorneys, and never play the role of this particular person's attorney. Once the individual has participated in the evaluation, the information cannot be kept confidential. Therefore, it would be unwise for the evaluator to attempt to persuade a hesitant subject who has not yet been advised by counsel to participate in the evaluation.

BEWARE Be careful not to give what might be construed as legal advice to the evaluee.

Competence

The evaluee's competence to proceed is generally irrelevant in cases of civil commitment. It is not unusual in conventional civil commitment cases for the person being evaluated to display active symptoms of severe mental illness, with such symptoms resulting in a threat to the safety of self or others. However, legislators and courts have apparently recognized that SVP evaluees are likely to be different in this regard. The identified disorder is much more likely to be a paraphilia or a personality disorder than a psychosis. Two states (Massachusetts and South Carolina) have specifically addressed the situation involving defendants who may be considered for SVP commitment after being found incompetent to proceed and not restorable on their most recent offense. Legislators have treated the most recent offense behavior as quite relevant to SVP proceedings. Therefore, specific procedures were implemented, in which the individual could be found to have committed the alleged offense—that is, be determined to be factually guilty even when they are not competent for trial—and SVP proceedings could then be conducted.

A second competence issue is whether a respondent can be committed through SVP proceedings when that respondent is not competent to testify, follow testimony, or understand the evidence being used by prosecutors. This situation was recently litigated in Texas, and the appellate court held that, considering the issue was civil and involved no punishment, it was no more necessary for SVP respondents to be competent in these areas than for any other person subject to civil commitment (*In re Fisher*, 2005). However, an earlier Florida court found that any offenders at risk for SVP commitment did need to be competent to testify and assist in their defense (*In re Branch*, 2004). Therefore, if practicing in a jurisdiction in which competence to proceed is required, or where the requirement is uncertain, it is best for evaluators to err on the side of caution. If it appears that the evaluee is potentially incompetent to proceed, it would be prudent to raise this issue with the source of the evaluator's appointment before proceeding with the assessment. Even better is to

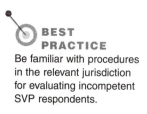

BEST PRACTICE
Be familiar with procedures in the relevant jurisdiction for evaluating incompetent SVP respondents.

know beforehand how to proceed with an SVP evaluation of an incompetent person in one's jurisdiction.

Right to Remain Silent

Whether an offender should be legally compelled to answer all questions posed in an SVP evaluation remains open to question. Melton et al. (2007) point out that courts have generally held that the Fifth Amendment is only binding in criminal proceedings. However, they also observe that a number of courts have applied the right to remain silent to civil procedures. Although SVP proceedings are officially considered civil rather than criminal, a number of jurisdictions have provided SVP evaluees with rights similar to those accorded criminal defendants. Florida case law stipulates that the individual must be competent to proceed prior to SVP consideration. A few states, such as Illinois, specifically grant the right to remain silent in SVP hearings.

The *Specialty Guidelines for Forensic Psychologists* indicate that psychologists should provide evaluees with information about their rights, the use to which any evaluation is apt to be put, and who will have access to it in the form of a notification given before the evaluation is begun (Committee on Ethical Guidelines for Forensic Psychologists, 1991).

Analogously, the *Ethical Guidelines for the Practice of Forensic Psychiatry* state: "At the outset of a face-to-face evaluation, notice should be given to the evaluee of the nature and purpose of the evaluation and the limits of its confidentiality" (American Academy of Psychiatry and Law, 2005, p. 2).

To ensure the evaluee's continued understanding of this information, it is common for evaluators to repeat it during the course of the evaluation to be as certain as possible that it is understood and remembered. This practice is based in part on the fundamental premise that the individual's privacy should not be invaded without the individual's permission (Melton et al., 2007). In jurisdictions or under circumstances in which there is no legal right to refuse participation, this repetition of information ensures at least the individual's awareness of the nature of the evaluation and the way in which it may be used (Heilbrun, 2001).

A cautious approach should be used toward probing or pressing for information directly from an individual respondent during an

BEWARE
Be cautious
when prob-
ing about unadjudicated
conduct, which may be
unverifiable or inadmissible.

interview. It might also give one pause about using queries such as, "Did you ever commit crimes as an adult and not get caught? What did you do?" (Hare, 2003, p. 26). While such information would clearly be relevant, it may not be verifiable. Particularly in the initial triage phase, the evaluee may not have the benefit of legal advice and may not fully comprehend any rights he may have. In the end, there may not be a clearly correct answer as to how much to probe in the interview for unadjudicated conduct. Such conduct is certainly relevant, although it is difficult (sometimes impossible) to verify. Probing for such conduct may increase the credibility of the evaluation, conveying the justifiable impression of thoroughness. However, unadjudicated conduct may not be admissible in an SVP hearing; whether such information is admissible is up to the judge.

Whatever approach an evaluator takes, it should be noted that evaluees are generally under considerable pressure to participate in the assessment and have no immunity against prosecution for additional offenses. In addition, Doren (2002) cautions against interpreting the behavior of an individual who does not wish to answer certain questions as deceitful or pathological, as there may be other reasons for such hesitancy (including anxiety or the advice of counsel). Some evaluators begin to address this issue in their initial disclosure, informing the individual that it is his choice whether to answer any or all of the questions posed, but adding that a report must be written regardless of participation.

Risk Management Recommendations

Heilbrun (1997) has proposed going beyond risk assessment to consider risk management. Risk assessment involves determining the level of risk presented by an individual for certain future behavior, whereas risk management includes strategies to reduce that risk. Risk assessment is often based primarily on static factors, whereas risk management involves more dynamic variables that are subject to change through intervention.

Under many of the current SVP statutes, a risk management plan may not be called for, as there are only two options for the decision maker: either commit the individual or release him without conditions. If committed, the person is apt to be confined in a secure facility for a lengthy period of time. The programming received will be left up to the staff of the facility providing treatment, and that facility will eventually be responsible for discharge recommendations. Some courts have openly concluded that risk should not be managed—it should be eliminated. The Supreme Court of Wisconsin recently considered whether conditions of release are relevant to the decision in SVP commitment proceedings. In this case, the justices found that the presence of a mental abnormality in an individual, and not some external consideration, was what the court should consider—making potential release conditions irrelevant (*In re Mark,* 2006). Even in Texas, where SVP commitment is outpatient only, there are 97 specific conditions universally mandated and monitored by the Council for Sex Offender Treatment.

Risk management is most relevant to the question of whether an individual who has been committed may be released under some conditions. The goal in answering this question would be to reduce the state's burden of housing individuals in secure facilities and allow the individual to function in the least restrictive environment, while at the same time protecting society from undue risk.

4
chapter

BEST PRACTICE
When risk management is a relevant issue, a best-practice risk management plan should be constructed in four steps.

Step 1.   Generate a list of factors, both nomothetic from the research data and idiographic based on the offender's history, relating to the individual's risk for reoffending.

Step 2.   Examine the factors to determine which of them are amenable to change through planned intervention.

Step 3.   Develop specific intervention strategies for each of these dynamic (potentially changeable) risk factors. For practical, cost-effective risk management plans, it is important that interventions be developed on a case-by-case basis and that one-size-fits-all models be avoided (Conroy, 2006).

Step 4.   Establish a review schedule so that future circumstances can be addressed, strategies can be added, and ineffective interventions can be dropped. (For a complete discussion of risk management planning see Conroy & Murrie, 2007.)

Collateral Information

Collateral information is a critical element in any scientifically grounded risk assessment, and is often much more important than information gained in a face-to-face interview (Conroy & Murrie, 2007). The type and amount of useful information will vary according to the stage of the proceedings at which the evaluation is conducted. Less information is typically available at the screening stage. Evaluations at this point often need to be conducted more quickly, and agencies do not wish to invest excessive amounts of time and money conducting investigations of numerous individuals who are unlikely to be subject to commitment proceedings. Most candidates in some jurisdictions have either been imprisoned or hospitalized immediately prior to the evaluation, so institution records function as a starting point. Whenever possible, records should be reviewed prior to interviewing the evaluee. This allows the evaluator to plan the focus of the interview and to note and pursue inconsistencies. Even during the initial stage of evaluation, clinicians should carefully note gaps in the records and observe when essential documents are unavailable.

Verification of Critical Information

Records—including those generated by government agencies and law enforcement personnel—vary greatly in quality, comprehensiveness, and accuracy. Given the very high stakes surrounding these evaluations, it is crucial that information critical to an opinion be carefully verified when possible and any lack of verification openly acknowledged (DeClue, 2006). Some records are dated, signed by the person responsible, and cite sources for the information. In the case of federal pre-sentence investigations, there is even a manual describing the regulations that must be followed in preparing these reports. Some records may appear official (e.g., on government letterhead, complete with the state seal), yet may contain information that has never been verified. When no source is noted for the information provided, it is entirely possible that it is simply an offender's self-report, provided during an interview on a prior occasion.

Two examples, given next, illustrate the problems that may be encountered with records. In

BEST PRACTICE
Review records prior to the interview and note any gaps in the information available.

the first, the evaluator obtained the official prison medical record of an offender.

The prison medical record indicated that the offender had suffered a severe head injury while playing football at age 14 and had been in a coma for several days. This was reportedly followed by 10 years of grand mal seizures, only partially controlled by Dilantin®. The individual had then been prescribed Dilantin® during his time in prison, and no further seizure activity was noted. It was later discovered that this information was obtained solely from the offender, had never been verified, and had never been assessed through current medical testing. The offender later admitted that he had fabricated the story to avoid being assigned to an outdoor detail in the hot sun.

A second example occurred in the context of an SVP evaluation.

The offender had recently been transferred from the correctional system in a distant state after completing his sentence there. The official record in his file stated that he had served time for raping an 80-year-old woman and a 40-year-old woman. However, when the record from the other jurisdiction was located, it appeared that his victims had been an 8-year-old girl and a 4-year-old girl. Clearly this would make a difference, both in potential diagnosis and in the analysis of significant risk factors (i.e., deviant interests). When the mistake was called to the attention of the erring department, it was labeled a "minor typographical error."

Evaluators must beware of relying heavily on any single source describing a significant risk factor that cannot be verified elsewhere—particularly if the individual denies it. Any concern about the reliability of collateral information used to form an opinion should be specifically acknowledged in the report.

Convictions, Charges, Accusations, and Self-Report

One of the most difficult tasks facing the forensic evaluator in an SVP assessment is determining what information is sufficiently reliable to form the basis for an opinion. According to the *Specialty Guidelines for Forensic Psychologists:* VI.F. (1) "When using hearsay data that have not been corroborated, but are nevertheless utilized, forensic psychologists have an affirmative responsibility to acknowledge the uncorroborated status of those data and the reasons for relying upon such data" (Committee on Ethical Guidelines for Forensic Psychologists, 1991, p. 662). Similarly, the *Ethical Guidelines for the Practice of Forensic Psychiatry* note that forensic evaluators must be objective and consider the reliability of the data:

> They communicate the honesty of their work, efforts to attain objectivity, and the soundness of their clinical opinion, by distinguishing, to the extent possible, between verified and unverified information as well as among clinical "facts," "inferences," and "impressions." (American Academy of Psychiatry and Law, 2005, p. 3)

It would not be unusual for records to contain information about convictions, charges that were dropped or not prosecuted for some reason, and accusations of various kinds. The offender may also describe acts not mentioned in the record. It can be argued that only offenses for which the individual has been convicted should be included in the history of sexual offending from which risk factors are derived. These acts, after all, have been proven beyond a reasonable doubt to have occurred. However, there is general agreement that use of only convictions is likely to significantly underestimate the offense history (Marques et al., 2005; Quinsey et al., 2006), thus minimizing the scope and intensity of important risk factors. This is the case for a number of reasons, discussed below.

REASONS WHY USE OF ONLY CONVICTIONS MAY UNDERESTIMATE OFFENSE HISTORY

- Prosecutors may have charged an individual with a number of similar offenses but only prosecuted one.
- Charges may have been dropped as part of a plea agreement, rather than for lack of evidence.
- As part of a plea agreement, charges may be changed to being nonsexual in nature, thus avoiding the registration requirement. For example, in one case, although details of the offense clearly indicated the rape of a 16-year-old

girl, the final agreed-upon charge was injury to a disabled person (her "disability" being defined as her age).

- Some of the most heinous offenses are often classified simply as homicide (Quinsey et al., 2006).

- Research has demonstrated that, given some type of immunity, offenders often admit to many more offenses than have been discovered (Abel et al., 1987; Doren, 1998).

In determining what is reasonable to rely on, evaluators should consider that this is officially a civil commitment. In more traditional commitment proceedings in which someone is judged to present a risk due to a major mental illness, the evaluee has often been neither convicted of nor charged with a criminal offense. Yet the petitioning clinician is expected to sort through the available evidence (which may be minimal or contradictory), determine what is credible, and form an opinion.

The task of the SVP evaluator can be conceptualized in much the same way. For example, consider the following case:

The offender was charged with eight counts of sexual assault of a child, each instance recorded on videotape by the offender and his accomplice, and each accompanied by detailed reports. The prosecution only pursued conviction on one count in this case.

An evaluator might consider this credible evidence of a pattern of sexually deviant behavior and would feel remiss in not including it in the analysis. Consider another instance:

A 45-year-old man is convicted of molesting two prepubescent boys repeatedly over several months. Despite the alleged history of repeated contact, the official charges are for two specific events. Then the offender tells the evaluator that he has molested more than 100 boys over the past 10 years; he says he kept records in a journal that he destroyed when his arrest was imminent.

The clinician in this case would probably judge that using only the two convictions would substantially minimize the actual conduct.

Other information might appear much less accurate. For example, the local sheriff's suspicions about the evaluee or the ex-wife's accusation during a custody battle of the evaluee molesting their child might not be sufficiently accurate to even mention, unless there is collateral information against which the evaluator might gauge the consistency of reports of this behavior. What one considers as adequately reliable is often not an easy decision. However, the court is always the final arbiter of what evidence may be considered. It is therefore essential that the mental health professional carefully describe all evidence considered, the supporting documentation, and the clinician's rationale for inclusion or exclusion. As we have suggested earlier, in some cases it may be possible and useful to express one's opinion conditionally. For example, if appropriate, an evaluator could state the following:

> If Mr. X only engaged in sexual violence twice in his life, as indicated by the convictions, then, in my opinion, there is not sufficient evidence to show that he is likely to engage in future acts of sexual violence. If, on the other hand, Mr. X actually engaged in sexual violence seven times as listed in the original charges, then it would be my opinion that he is likely to commit new acts of sexual violence if he is released. I defer to the trier of fact to decide whether Mr. X actually engaged in sexual violence more often than is reflected in his convictions.

This conditional stance is particularly useful when the evaluee denies having committed the offense or offenses of which he has been convicted (or to which he has pled guilty)—not an uncommon position for evaluees to take, in our experience. We recommend that the evaluator make clear what facts she is assuming as a basis for a finding and leave to the court the determination of what facts are sufficiently reliable.

Medical Records

In some jurisdictions access to an individual's medical records may require informed consent from the evaluee, and this may be difficult to obtain. Other jurisdictions, by contrast, are very liberal with rules granting such access in these cases. In these jurisdictions, comprehensive records (medical and otherwise) are provided as a matter of course. Local customs vary greatly in this regard. For example, North Dakota's SVP law specifies that neither

BEST PRACTICE

Always describe your reasons for including information in the report and for considering it reliable.

physician–patient privilege nor psychotherapist–patient privilege applies to records considered relevant in these proceedings. One alternative, available in most jurisdictions, would be to request that records be court ordered. Once again, in such instances, practice guidelines emphasize the importance of knowing and following the rules of a particular jurisdiction.

> VI. B.(1) Documentation of the data upon which one's evidence is based is subject to the normal rules of discovery, disclosure, confidentiality, and privilege that operate in the jurisdiction in which the data were obtained. Forensic psychologists have an obligation to be aware of those rules and to regulate their conduct in accordance with them. (Committee on Ethical Guidelines for Forensic Psychologists, 1991, p. 661)

Special Ethical Concerns

Ethical dilemmas may arise in any forensic mental health assessment. They have been considered in every step of the preparation process discussed in this chapter. However, four additional areas merit special attention: conflicts of interest, use of treatment records, consent and disclosure, and uncooperative evaluees.

Conflicts of Interest

The *Specialty Guidelines for Forensic Psychologists* universally warn psychologists to exercise care in avoiding any foreseeable conflict of interest (Committee on Ethical Guidelines for Forensic Psychologists, 1991, p. 659). This is in keeping with current APA standard 3.05(a):

> A psychologist refrains from entering into a multiple relationship if the multiple relationship could reasonably be expected to impair the psychologist's objectivity, competence, or effectiveness in performing his or her functions as a psychologist, or otherwise risks exploitation or harm to the person with whom the professional relationship exists. (American Psychological Association, 2002, p. 1065)

This would, of course, preclude a psychologist from performing an evaluation in any case in which there was a prior relationship with the offender, victims, or anyone else closely connected with this case.

4
chapter

Potential conflicts could also arise if the clinician had previously been involved in evaluating the offender. The guidelines also address conflicts with regard to personal values:

> III. E. Forensic psychologists recognize that their own personal values, moral beliefs, or personal and professional relationships with parties to a legal proceeding may interfere with their ability to practice competently. Under such circumstances, forensic psychologists are obligated to decline participation or to limit their assistance in a manner consistent with professional obligations. (Committee on Ethical Guidelines for Forensic Psychologists, 1991, p. 658)

Sexual offenses—particularly those perpetrated against children—are often especially offensive to people's moral values. If the evaluator has been a victim or in some way connected to a victim of such an offense, this history can trigger a conflict of interest, even when the current evaluee was not involved. This is an issue for clinicians to consider before accepting a referral.

By far the most prominent conflict of interests in this arena involves the roles of therapist and forensic evaluator. Although some (e.g., Helzel, 2007) would disagree, most of what is written in forensic psychology and forensic psychiatry underscores the point that playing the roles of both therapist and forensic evaluator in the same case presents a serious dual-role problem (Bersoff, 2003; Greenberg & Shuman, 1997, 2007; Strasberger, Gutheil, & Brodsky, 1997). A number of state licensing boards have endorsed this position as well (Bush, Connell, & Denney, 2006). In one context, the client is the patient receiving treatment; in the other, the client is the attorney or the court. Therapists typically try to function in the best interests of their patients, whereas forensic evaluators must strive to be objective and unbiased. In the former context, the patient is promised confidentiality with few exceptions; in the latter, confidentiality generally does not exist. The *Guidelines for the Practice of Forensic Psychiatry* advise against mixing therapeutic and forensic evaluations roles, as follows:

> Psychiatrists who take on a forensic role for patients they are treating may adversely affect the therapeutic relationship with them. Forensic evaluations usually require interviewing corroborative

sources, exposing information to public scrutiny, or subjecting evaluees and the treatment itself to potentially damaging cross-examination. The forensic evaluation and the credibility of the practitioner may also be undermined by conflicts inherent in the differing clinical and forensic roles. Treating psychiatrists should therefore generally avoid acting as an expert witness for their patients or performing evaluations of their patients for legal purposes. (American Academy of Psychiatry and Law, 2005, p. 3)

As a therapist, the practitioner uses empathy to form a strong therapeutic alliance. As a forensic evaluator, the clinician maintains stricter boundaries, informing the evaluee that no treatment or other support services will be provided. Therapists generally rely heavily on information received from their patient, whereas forensic evaluators attempt to verify every important piece of information using collateral sources.

Despite the clear conflict in roles, it is common for those providing treatment to sexual offenders in the community to be asked to share most, if not all, information from the treatment with legal authorities, and to perform regular risk assessments. Under such arrangements, the therapist must waive therapeutic confidentiality and rely heavily on outside information. The therapist is also placed in the odd position of evaluating the effectiveness of her own work: Based on the therapy received, has this individual become a lower risk for further offending? The more frequently mental health professionals agree to accept the roles of both therapist and risk assessor in the same case, the more prevalent this practice is likely to become. Those who encourage this practice would argue that the total waiver of confidentiality and therapists being an integral part of the risk assessment process are essential to a full "containment approach."

Under this philosophy, programs apply every possible intervention routinely in every case, with the goal of promoting public safety. Some empirical data have begun to appear examining results of the approach as a

4 chapter

INFO

Potential conflicts of interest include the following:

- Multiple relationships
- Interference of personal values
- Dual roles of therapist and forensic evaluator

BEWARE
Be cautious of assertions that open communication between therapists and law enforcement staff is essential to treatment effectiveness.

whole. For example, Stalans (2004) did follow-up research in three Illinois counties and found some mildly encouraging results using this strategy. However, to date, no studies have distinguished the individual elements of the approach to determine which are specifically responsible for the outcome and which may be having the opposite effect. Although probation officers surveyed endorse the importance of complete, open communication between therapists and law enforcement staff (English, Pullen & Jones, 1996), no study has actually tested this hypothesis (Conroy, 2006).

The Use of Treatment Records

Even if general medical records are held confidential, it is likely that sex offender treatment program records, particularly from programs housed in correctional institutions, will be made readily available. This is partly a response to the U.S. Supreme Court decision in *McKune v. Lile* (2002), involving a suit by a prison inmate assigned to a treatment program for sexual offenders. Program participants were required to make admissions regarding past sexual conduct and take total responsibility for that conduct; otherwise, sanctions could be applied by the prison system—including loss of privileges and transfer to a more secure facility. The plaintiff contended that this violated his Fifth Amendment rights, as he was being coerced into making admissions that could later be used against him in a court of law. However, the Court held that he was entitled to no immunity and that the program, as structured, met a reasonable correctional objective.

Even when records of such treatment are not requested, they may be forwarded to the evaluator as collateral information. They may contain some important insights and information to be explored. However, the forensic clinician

CASE LAW
McKune v. Lile
(2002)

● The U.S. Supreme Court held that the SVP inmate was entitled to no immunity.

● The Court allowed a treatment program to require admissions of past sexual conduct.

BEWARE
The circum-
stances under which data in
medical records were
obtained may make their
validity questionable.

should keep in mind the circumstances under which the information was obtained. If, for example, the treatment reports are based on unstructured clinical judgments, these observations may be of questionable validity. If admissions are made to meet program requirements, it is also possible that they lack veracity.

Other less specific medical or mental health records may be sought as part of an SVP evaluation. However, according to the *Specialty Guidelines for Forensic Psychologists*, it is important for evaluators to "make every effort to maintain confidentiality with regard to any information that does not bear directly upon the legal purpose of the evaluation" (Committee on Ethical Guidelines for Forensic Psychologists, 1991, p. 660). Similarly, the *Ethical Guidelines for the Practice of Forensic Psychiatry* state:

> Respect for the individual's right of privacy and the maintenance of confidentiality should be major concerns when performing forensic evaluations. Psychiatrists should maintain confidentiality to the extent possible, given the legal context. (American Academy of Psychiatry and the Law, 2005, p. 1)

4
chapter

If a record is provided by one of the parties, it is generally the evaluator's obligation to review it. However, it may be unnecessary to seek out confidential medical information that is apt to have little relevance to the task at hand—particularly if the evaluator has determined that there are no identifiable gaps in the information already obtained. Doren (2002) encouraged the use of judgment regarding the never-ending search for records, noting, "Sometimes 'more' is just 'more' and not really of any use" (p. 33).

Consent and Disclosure

The *Ethical Principles of Psychologists and Code of Conduct* (American Psychological Association, 2002), *Specialty Guidelines for Forensic Psychologists* (Committee on Ethical Guidelines for Forensic Psychologists, 1991), and *Ethical Guidelines for the Practice of Forensic Psychiatry*

BEST PRACTICE
Maintain confidentiality of information that is irrelevant to the legal context.

INFO

Checklist for Informed Consent:

- Identity of evaluator
- Evaluator's employer in the case
- Procedures to be used
- Limits of confidentiality
- No treatment services will be provided
- Access to evaluation records

(American Academy of Psychiatry and the Law, 2005) are consistent in the following SGFP specification regarding consent and disclosure:

V. B. Forensic psychologists inform their clients of the limits of confidentiality of their services and their products by providing them with an understandable statement of their rights, privileges, and the limitations of confidentiality. (Committee on Ethical Guidelines for Forensic Psychologists, 1991, p. 660)

INFORMED CONSENT

Unless an evaluation is court ordered or otherwise mandated by law, informed consent of the evaluee is required. This includes a full explanation of the identity of the evaluator, by whom he is employed, the purpose of the evaluation, procedures that will be used, and the limits of confidentiality. The evaluee should also be told that no treatment services will be provided by the evaluator, and that absent a court order, the evaluee will only have access to the evaluation records through his attorney. Once the information has been provided, and the evaluator is satisfied that it has been understood, the evaluee must knowingly and voluntarily consent to the assessment.

IV. E. (1) If the client appears unwilling to proceed after receiving a thorough notification of the purposes, methods, and intended uses of the forensic evaluation, the evaluation should be postponed and the psychologist should take steps to place the client in contact with his/her attorney for the purpose of legal advice on the issue of participation. (Committee on Ethical Guidelines for Forensic Psychologists, 1991, p. 659)

The American Association of Psychiatry and Law has similar guidelines for forensic psychiatrists in this regard (American Association of Psychiatry and Law, 2005).

DISCLOSURE

In practice, many SVP evaluations conducted by psychologists are either court ordered or mandated by law. Therefore, disclosure (also called "notification of purpose," but not informed consent) is required. The evaluator must still make every effort to explain to the evaluee all of the elements of the evaluation procedure listed above. However, the evaluee should be informed that the evaluation will be completed regardless of whether consent is provided.

If it is possible to identify the attorney for the evaluee prior to beginning the evaluation, it is often helpful to share the disclosure form intended to be used so that the attorney may discuss it with his client prior to any interview. This may minimize the evaluee's tendency to direct legal questions or requests for legal advice to the evaluator. It may also minimize the potential for an evaluee's uncertainty about whether to participate in the interview. The *Ethical Guidelines for Forensic Psychiatrists*, in its commentary, handles this situation as follows:

> It is important to appreciate that in particular situations, such as court-ordered evaluations for competency to stand trial or involuntary commitment, neither assent nor informed consent is required. In such cases, psychiatrists should inform the evaluee that if the evaluee refuses to participate in the evaluation, this fact may be included in any report or testimony. If the evaluee does not appear capable of understanding the information provided regarding the evaluation, this impression should also be included in any report and, when feasible, in testimony. (American Academy of Psychiatry and Law, 2005, p. 2)

THIRD PARTIES

Third parties are often interviewed by forensic evaluators as part of the SVP evaluation process. They are also entitled to disclosure of the identity of the evaluator and by whom she is employed, the purpose of the evaluation, procedures that will be used, and the limits of

INFO

Language such as the following is commonly used in disclosure forms: "I further understand it is up to me whether I answer any or all of the questions posed by the evaluator. However, if I do not participate, the evaluator must nonetheless complete a report based upon available records and other collateral information."

BEWARE
Never
assume that
sources of collateral information are aware of the lack
of confidentiality.

confidentiality. They should also be told that any information provided may be included in the evaluator's report and/or testimony, and that the source of that information will be identified. It should never be assumed that sources of collateral information—including physicians and other mental health professionals—are aware of the lack of confidentiality in the forensic context.

The Uncooperative Evaluee

Every evaluator will encounter evaluees who refuse to participate or are only minimally cooperative in the SVP evaluation process. Regardless of the individual's initial attitude, clinicians should at least attempt an interview. If feasible, it is best that the clinician personally approach the potential evaluee, provide the person with full disclosure, and document that individual's response. However, it should also be noted that it is not the mental health professional's responsibility to persuade, or in any way pressure, the person to cooperate. Decisions on the extent of cooperation should be left to the individual and his legal counsel. Some psychologists are very uncomfortable with the idea of completing an evaluation absent a personal interview with the individual being evaluated. However, the *Special Guidelines for Forensic Psychologists* addresses this issue:

> VI. H. Forensic psychologists avoid giving written or oral evidence about the psychological characteristics of particular individuals when they have not had an opportunity to conduct an examination of the individual adequate to the scope of the statements, opinions, or conclusions to be issued. Forensic psychologists make every reasonable effort to conduct such examinations. When it is not possible or feasible to do so, they make clear the impact of such limitations on the reliability and validity of their professional products, evidence, or testimony. (Committee on Ethical Guidelines for Forensic Psychologists, 1991, p. 663)

The *Ethical Guidelines for the Practice of Forensic Psychiatry* come to a similar conclusion (American Academy of Psychiatry and Law, 2005).

BEWARE
Make a
reasonable
effort to obtain an interview,
but do not try to persuade or
pressure individuals to
cooperate in the evaluation.

In the SVP arena, the basis for many of the conclusions is more likely to be drawn from records and other collateral information than from the interview. As noted earlier, it is relatively rare for those subject to SVP evaluations to suffer from major mental disorders requiring extensive interviewing or psychological testing. The three most common diagnostic categories are paraphilias, personality disorders, and substance abuse. For the most part, these are chronic conditions that are not dependent upon current mental status, and records should provide valuable information. Any risk assessment will rely heavily on collateral information that has been carefully verified. Both the PCL-R and most relevant actuarial assessment instruments can be completed from a detailed, accurate record. Therefore, it is likely that well-grounded information and opinions can be provided without the benefit of an interview. However, it is essential that evaluators note the absence of personal contact, efforts made to obtain it, and limitations this may have on the information and opinions offered.

The ethical concerns discussed here are neither exhaustive nor prescriptive. However, they are issues that arise with great frequency for individuals involved in this work. It is helpful, particularly for novice SVP evaluators, to give these issues careful consideration in preparing to conduct SVP evaluations.

chapter **4**

Data Collection | 5

In this chapter, we will discuss the major aspects of data collection. Although each evaluator has her particular style of collecting evaluation data, we recommend a general sequence. First, the evaluator should review the file to orient herself to the background on the case. The file review alerts the evaluator to particular areas of inquiry that are needed to reach conclusions concerning the psycholegal questions. A thorough file review can also lead the evaluator to generate a list of hypotheses, which the interview can assist in testing. After reviewing the file, the evaluator will interview the evaluee (assuming that the evaluee is willing to be interviewed, which is not always the case). The evaluator may then choose to review the results of psychological tests, which can be administered either before or after the interview. At some point, depending on availability, the evaluator may interview collateral sources, such as institutional staff (to obtain information on the offender's institutional behavior) or others familiar with the individual's history outside of the institution.

File Review

The first step in evaluating an SVP commitment case is reviewing the files, which can be voluminous. Given the focus on the evaluee's entire life (some diagnoses involve inferences about adolescent or childhood adjustment), there is virtually no limit to the historical information that can be relevant in these cases. Also, SVP evaluees may be uncooperative with or decline to participate in an interview. Therefore, the evaluator may need to rely on archival data more than would otherwise be the case in providing a foundation for his inferences.

In some jurisdictions, the evaluee has already been temporarily committed pending a final commitment hearing. In such cases, the file from the evaluee's civil commitment facility will be available. From this file, the evaluator can assess the evaluee's recent institutional adjustment through work, housing, and therapy reports. If the evaluee has institutional charges, these should be evident.

If the evaluee is being considered for transfer to a civil commitment facility, the most common time for the evaluation is toward the end of the evaluee's incarceration. In these cases, the evaluator has access to the file from the evaluee's most recent incarceration. If the evaluee has been previously incarcerated, then frequently the evaluator will have access to records from previous incarcerations in the same state as well. By reviewing these files, the evaluator can assess both recent and past institutional adjustment, as well as cooperation with and progress in treatment, if treatment was made available to the evaluee.

The more thoroughly the evaluator can review the file, the better she will be prepared to interview the evaluee (and later testify, if necessary). SVP commitment cases require the evaluator to make a number of inferences about three psycholegal constructs relevant to this referral: mental abnormality, volitional impairment, and increased risk. Such inferences may be subject to vigorous cross-examination. Consequently, the firmer a foundation the evaluator has through a file review, the better the evaluator will be able to interview the evaluee, articulate foundational facts and inferences in the report, and testify in a commitment hearing.

INFO

Primary documents may include the following:

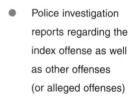

● Police investigation reports regarding the index offense as well as other offenses (or alleged offenses)

● Witness statements

● Evaluee's prior statement(s) to law enforcement or treatment staff

● Child protection service agency investigation reports

● Criminal history record

Primary Documents

Ideally, the institutional file will contain "raw data" for the evaluation. These documents provide the original information from which the evaluee's life history can be reconstructed. Such documents can be considered "primary," given that they involve direct reporting by some observer (or participant).

Secondary Documents

In addition, there are "secondary documents" in the file. These are one level removed from the primary documents and involve information obtained from a primary document. For example, whereas a police report would be considered a primary document, a pre-sentence investigation report that summarizes police reports would be considered a secondary document. Sometimes documents have both primary and secondary aspects. For instance, a prior psychiatric hospital intake report that provides a diagnosis at the time of intake is a primary document in that regard, but if the document also summarizes historical records of previous mental health treatment or diagnoses, it would be considered a secondary document concerning those areas. Secondary documents may be helpful in establishing a history of prior diagnoses or prior court findings of fact upon which the evaluator can rely in making a present diagnosis. Secondary documents sometimes include

INFO

Secondary documents may include the following:

- A child protection agency summary of an evaluee's history of involvement with that agency

- A pre-sentence investigation report that provides a summary of the evaluee's relevant life history, including areas such as employment, education, and substance abuse

- Prior psychological or psychiatric evaluations (to the extent that these summarize or draw conclusions about historical patterns of unobserved behaviors)

- Prior school records, particularly if the evaluee had been a student classified as having special needs and therefore was psychologically evaluated by the child study team

5
chapter

BEWARE
When relying on secondary documents, focus on supporting data and not on the conclusions of others.

conclusions, such as the document author's opinion on the meaning of certain facts—for example, a child protection agency's conclusion as to whether abuse or neglect occurred.

Although secondary documents may be helpful, the evaluator should be careful not to rely on them too heavily in the absence of primary documents. Many times, the reasons for prior diagnoses or findings are not articulated in secondary documents. Thus, it may be difficult to determine the foundation for the opinions in those documents. If the secondary documents clearly state the facts or observations upon which the inferences or conclusions are based, then these documents can be invaluable in providing historical information that may be available nowhere else. The evaluator should treat the reports of other experts in the same way as he treats other collateral data—with interest in their observations but not their conclusions. The evaluator must draw his own conclusions based on all of the available data. Because the focus is really on the basis for the previous expert's conclusions and not the conclusions themselves, secondary documents without supporting data hold little value for the evaluator.

Courts vary in the extent to which mental health experts can rely on secondary documents; however, expert witnesses are allowed to rely on less reliable information, including hearsay, if it is the type of information upon which one ordinarily relies in one's professional work. If possible, the evaluator should rely as much as possible on verifiable primary sources. As DeClue (2006, p. 122) states:

> Similarly, forensic evaluators must consider the facts carefully before rendering an opinion. We should rely on primary documents (such as the arrest reports, witness statements, sworn statements at trial or deposition, and official court records such as judgments and sentences). When primary documents are not available, we should request them. On those occasions when the primary documents are ultimately unavailable, we should a) clearly present the limitations of the data if we express an opinion, and b) refrain from expressing an opinion when there [are] insufficient reliable data to support one. Meanwhile, we must recognize that other professionals may have inadvertently presented a non-fact as a fact, whether by reporting unchecked statements by the offender or via simple mistakes or carelessness.

Conducting Interviews with Evaluees

At the beginning of the interview, consistent with other forensic evaluations, the evaluator should obtain informed consent from the evaluee. In the case of court-ordered or statutorily mandated evaluations, evaluators should provide disclosure or notification.

Issue of Incompetent to Consent

Of course, the evaluee's ability to consent is presumed in the above recommendations. If the evaluee is incompetent to consent, the evaluator must be aware of the legal context in his jurisdiction in determining whether to proceed. In the case of an SVP examination, the evaluator may be legally allowed to proceed. For example, if the evaluation is court ordered or mandated by statute, then the evaluee's consent is not required. If the evaluation is requested by the defense attorney, not proceeding because of incompetence to consent may prevent the defense attorney from adequately representing the evaluee.

For example, suppose that a court-appointed evaluator recommends SVP commitment, and the defense attorney requests a rebuttal evaluation. The evaluator meets with the client and then tells the attorney, "I don't think he's competent to consent to participate in this evaluation." The defense attorney replies, "But he participated in the previous one, and I'm asking for this one—can't we proceed on this basis?" We believe the answer to that question should be yes, for the same reason that one can evaluate juveniles upon the request

BEST PRACTICE
Before starting an interview:

- Explain the purpose of the evaluation, the use to which the evaluation will be put, and the individuals, agencies, and/or court to whom the evaluation report will be sent.

- Clearly explain the limits of confidentiality.

- Ask the evaluee to paraphrase the explanation, to ensure that the evaluee understands these parameters of the evaluation.

- Encourage the evaluee to ask any questions or raise any concerns he may have regarding the evaluation process.

- Carefully document the information provided to the evaluee, the extent to which it appeared to be understood, and (if consent is relevant) whether consent was provided.

BEST PRACTICE
Unless local law prohibits it, we recommend continuing the evaluation in cases in which informed consent is not required, but documenting the aspects of the notification in which the evaluee was deficient. In situations in which local law indicates that consent is required, we recommend that both attorneys be notified so that the matter can be resolved by the court, perhaps with a court order to proceed.

of their attorneys but without permission from their parent or guardian.

On this issue of competence, as with all others, the evaluator should be aware of local laws. For example, a Florida court (*In re Branch,* 2004) found that an individual must be competent to proceed in order to participate in an SVP proceeding. However, this finding may not apply in the jurisdiction in which the evaluator is practicing. There is no specific competency entitled "competency to participate in a forensic evaluation." If such a competency did exist, how many acutely psychotic individuals would ever be evaluated for a variety of outcomes?

Essential Constructs

In conducting an interview, it is helpful to be guided by an understanding of the information necessary to answer the relevant psycholegal questions. The three related constructs of mental abnormality, volitional impairment, and elevated risk are discussed in detail in Chapter 2. The evaluator's job is to gather information that would enable her to reach conclusions about these constructs, so the interview must cover areas needed to establish a foundation. Although these constructs generally apply throughout the United States, the evaluator should also be aware of statutory and case law that might highlight particular areas of inquiry relevant to a determination of SVP civil commitment in her jurisdiction.

Relevant History

The evaluator should take a relevant history from the evaluee. This is useful in determining whether the evaluee has a mental abnormality, because one would expect evidence of this to be present in the individual's history. The evaluator should inquire about the evaluee's sexual history in detail, because the evaluee's ability to control his sexual urges and behaviors is critical to an SVP commitment. (Later, we suggest some structured guides that may be helpful in systematically sampling the various areas of the evaluee's life history.) However, a sex offender evaluee may be less than forthcoming during an interview about his history. There are emotional reasons, such as embarrassment, that might lead the evaluee to minimize the extent of prior life difficulties. There are also legal reasons that might lead the evaluee to minimize past difficulties. The evaluee may realize (or perhaps be advised by his attorney) that acknowledgement of prior life difficulties, sexual and otherwise, may make it more likely that he will be civilly committed. Consequently, the interview should be treated as only one source of data, and not necessarily the most accurate one. The evaluator should rely on collateral sources, such as a thorough records review, to cross-check the interview data. Hare (2003, p. 19) suggests the following in assessing antisocial characteristics through an interview:

> Occasionally, there are large discrepancies between the interview and collateral information. If it is possible to determine that one source of information is more credible than the other, then greater weight is given to information from the more credible source. Otherwise, preference is given to the source most suggestive of psychopathy, on the assumption that the majority of people tend to under-report or minimize traits and behaviors that are characteristic of the disorder.

On this point, DeClue (personal communication, November 28, 2006) suggests "that an evaluator should take a moment to consider all of the available information in the case *with no consideration whatsoever to the respondent's statements at any time to anyone.* It is useful to see what is actually known without the respondent's self-serving statements. The evaluator may ultimately decide to give some weight to at least some of the respondent's statements, but, again, I highly recommend that the evaluator take a good, hard look at the known facts without the respondent's spin on them, and not lose sight of that picture" [emphasis in original].

Common Diagnoses and Broad Factors

Although any diagnosis could hypothetically suffice as a foundation for mental abnormality, in practice, two diagnoses are most common—antisocial personality disorder (and its extreme

BEWARE Individuals may downplay the extent of prior difficulties. Treat the interview as just one source of information.

variant, psychopathy) and some form of paraphilia. These two diagnoses parallel the two broad factors believed to generally elevate risk of sex offending: sexual deviance and general criminality or psychopathy (Doren, 2004). Although psychopathy is not a *DSM* diagnosis, it is a personality disorder with extensive empirical foundation that research has shown to be related to reoffense risk. Therefore, it is particularly important in the interview to obtain information concerning these two broad areas. Information from the interview (and, of course, the file review) will form the basis for inferences regarding the relevant mental health constructs.

Because the first area that the evaluator must cover in the interview is information needed to determine whether the evaluee has a mental abnormality, in practice, this determination requires either a *DSM* diagnosis, such as antisocial personality disorder or paraphilia, or a finding of psychopathy. Particularly for assessing antisocial personality disorder, the taking of a careful history is important, because this diagnosis requires a consideration of childhood and adolescent adjustment. To assess for a paraphilia, of course, sexual history is most relevant. However, sexual history is also relevant to antisocial personality disorder or psychopathy, since impulsivity and irresponsibility may be reflected in the evaluee's having had a large number of casual sexual partners. The Psychopathy Checklist-Revised (PCL-R, Hare) includes "promiscuous sexual behavior" as one of 20 areas being assessed.

Defining a Mental Disorder

With regard to a mental disorder, generally, the evaluator may take a broad approach in gathering information, following the *DSM-IV-TR*'s definition of a mental disorder:

> [E]ach of the mental disorders is conceptualized as a clinically significant behavioral or psychological syndrome or pattern that occurs in an individual and that is associated with present distress (e.g., a

painful symptom) or disability (i.e., impairment in one or more important areas of functioning) or with a significantly increased risk of suffering death, pain, disability, or an important loss of freedom. In addition, this syndrome or pattern must not be merely an expectable and culturally sanctioned response to a particular event, for example, the death of a loved one. Whatever its original cause, it must currently be considered a manifestation of a behavioral, psychological, or biological dysfunction in the individual. Neither deviant behavior (e.g., political, religious, or sexual) nor conflicts that are primarily between the individual and society are mental disorders unless the deviance or conflict is a symptom of a dysfunction in the individual, as described above. (American Psychiatric Association, 2000, xxxi)

Under this broad definition, the evaluator can gather information on whether the person has shown a clinically significant behavioral pattern that is associated with a significantly increased risk of suffering an important loss of freedom, that is, incarceration. A reasonable reading of the above quote suggests that a person who repeatedly engages in a pattern of behavior that results in the person being deprived of freedom (arrested, convicted, incarcerated) on multiple occasions meets the criteria for a mental disorder, with specific exceptions such as political dissent, exercise of a minority religion, or victimless sexual "crimes" (e.g., consensual adult sodomy).

However, as we noted in Chapter 2, legal definitions of mental disorder and clinical definitions of mental disorder flow from different traditions and do not necessarily match one another. The *DSM-IV-TR* itself addresses this issue, acknowledging the "imperfect fit between the questions of ultimate concern to the law and the information contained in a clinical diagnosis" (American Psychiatric Association, 2000, xxxiii).

In fact, in SVP evaluations, a *DSM* diagnosis is neither necessary nor sufficient. There must be an explicit connection between the mental disorder and an increased likelihood of sexual reoffending. This is the specific functional impairment required.

Methods for Obtaining a Diagnosis

A number of methods are available to the evaluator in obtaining information from the evaluee to reach a diagnosis. There are various structured interview protocols available for reaching both

5
chapter

The SVR-20 samples the following:

Psychosocial adjustment

1. Sexual deviation
2. Victim of child abuse
3. Psychopathy
4. Major mental illness
5. Substance use problems
6. Suicidal or homicidal ideation
7. Relationship problems
8. Employment problems
9. Past nonviolent offenses
10. Past violent offenses
11. Past supervision failure

Sexual offenses

12. High-density sex offenses
13. Multiple sex offense types
14. Physical harm to victim(s) in sex offenses
15. Use of weapons or threats of death in sex offenses
16. Escalation in frequency or severity of sex offenses
17. Extreme minimization or denial of sex offenses
18. Attitudes that support or condone sex offenses

Future plans

19. Lack of realistic plans
20. Negative attitude toward intervention

DSM Axis I and Axis II diagnoses, and some commentators believe that the use of such structured interviews increases reliability of the conclusions (see, for example, Rogers, 2001; Rogers & Shuman, 2005, p. 348). We do not recommend one particular method over another. The evaluator should use her professional judgment in deciding whether to use a structured interview and should be prepared to explain this choice when and if cross-examined. The determining factor should be how best to obtain the accurate, detailed information necessary to form opinions on the three relevant psycholegal constructs. However, the evaluator should be aware that some structured interviews, such as the PCL-R interview, have been designed specifically for forensic situations, and such interviews may well provide a helpful format for SVP evaluations, given their forensic nature.

However, there are advantages to using a structured procedure to guide one's interview (and file review). If that structured procedure has empirical support, then the evaluator's opinions will have a firmer foundation. Moreover, the use of a consistent structure for interview and file review will increase the transparency of the evaluation, making clear the areas that the evaluator is sampling and the inferences the evaluator is drawing. Finally, use of a structured,

empirically supported procedure allows
one to follow a coherent model in both
obtaining information and organizing
one's findings.

One approach, which we provide as
an example, is the use of an empirically
validated structured professional judgment tool, such as the Sexual Violence
Risk–20 (SVR-20; Boer, Hart, Kropp, &
Webster, 1997). Although the SVR-20
was developed from a review of existing
studies and not from an original, empirical study, subsequent research has found

its predictive power to be at least as good as actuarially developed scales
(DeClue, 2004; de Vogel, de Ruiter, van Beek, & Mead, 2004; Hanson
& Morton-Bourgon, 2004).

We recommend that the SVP evaluator consider using an empirically supported, structured instrument to guide his evaluation (see box
and further discussion of advantages and disadvantages toward the end
of this chapter). We leave the choice of which specific instrument (or
instruments) to use to the evaluator. This is a rapidly evolving area of
research and practice. New instruments are being developed regularly
and new studies on existing instruments are published in virtually every
issue of the relevant journals (such as *Law and Human Behavior;
Psychology, Public Policy and Law; Sexual Abuse: A Journal of Research
and Treatment; Behavioral Sciences and the Law; Criminal Justice and
Behavior; Journal of the American Academy of Psychiatry and the Law;*
and *Journal of Psychiatry and Law*).

Jurisdiction Requirements

Some jurisdictions require that specific questions be addressed or that
specific information be obtained. For example,
Texas, by statute, requires an assessment of psychopathy, so use of the PCL-R is standard (given
that it is considered the best-validated current
measure of this construct). California has a
detailed SVP evaluation manual and requires

**BEST
PRACTICE**
Be prepared to explain during
cross-examination your
choice of whether to use a
structured interview.

that the following areas be addressed (California Department of Mental Health, 2004, p. 20):

- Brief developmental history
- Psychiatric history
- Substance abuse history
- Juvenile and adult criminal history
- Parole history
- Institutional history
- Psychosexual history
- Relationship history
- Mental Status Examination, behavioral observations and attitudes of the inmate
- Psychiatric diagnosis in list format on Axis I and Axis II
- Explanation of psychiatric diagnosis offered
- Justification for the psychiatric diagnosis

In addition, academic history can provide useful indicators of early-onset antisocial behavior, relevant for a diagnosis of antisocial personality disorder. Many of these historical items bear on the development, trajectory, severity, and chronicity of antisocial behavior, all of which are critical for assessing antisocial personality disorder or psychopathy.

PCL-R Interview Guide

The PCL-R is accompanied by an interview guide (Hare, 2003) that systematically samples a variety of relevant areas (see box). The comprehensiveness of this guide makes it a reasonable choice for a semistructured interview. The resulting interview might provide sufficient information regarding general history to make a diagnosis of antisocial personality disorder or psychopathy. The primary reason that such an interview might not provide sufficient information to reach this diagnosis is the obvious one—lack of candor by the evaluee. Consequently, the evaluator may need to rely heavily on other sources of information. In fact, according the PCL-R manual, one cannot administer this measure without access to collateral data

INFO

The PCL-R interview guide covers the following areas:

- School history
- Work experience
- Career goals
- Finances
- Mental health history
- Family history
- Friends and intimate relationships
- Substance abuse and impulsive behaviors
- Anger control and emotions
- Antisocial behaviors
- General questions (e.g., self-esteem, empathy)

(for the very reason we describe). In addition, if the evaluator uses the PCL-R interview, he will want to augment it with questions focused on sexual behavior and diagnoses other than psychopathy.

Paraphilias

The second of the major diagnostic areas associated with SVP civil commitments is the paraphilias. To reach a diagnosis in this area, the sexual history is most relevant. Although it may be difficult to obtain accurate sexual history information from the evaluee, the evaluator should attempt to do so. This will involve comparing the interview results with materials available from the records, including the evaluee's admissions from prior evaluations.

As the evaluator is taking a sexual history from the evaluee, the evaluator should incorporate the diagnostic criteria for the paraphilias. This will help ensure that she obtains adequate information to determine whether paraphilias are present. Keeping a copy of the *DSM-IV-TR* criteria for paraphilia or devising and using one's own summary of these diagnostic criteria as an interview guide can facilitate thorough coverage of this area, because no structured interviews for diagnosing paraphilias currently exist.

5
chapter

Refusal to Participate

At times, an evaluee will decline to participate in the evaluation. The evaluee may believe (or have been advised by his attorney) that it is fruitless, or perhaps even damaging, to cooperate with an evaluation and will therefore refuse

BEST PRACTICE

Take note of diagnostic criteria for the paraphilias when taking a sexual history from the evaluee.

INFO

Areas sampled in the paraphilias section of the interview include the following:

- Early sexual experiences and interests
- Number and context of sexual partners
- Paraphilic sexual behavior
- Indicators of sexual self-control difficulties (e.g., extensive pornography use, prostitute use)
- History of illegal sexual activity, charged and otherwise

to be interviewed or take any psychological tests. In a similar though not identical context, the U.S. Supreme Court decided that there is no Fifth Amendment right against self-incrimination in a prison-based sex offender treatment program (*McKune v. Lile*, 2002). Although the circumstances are not identical and there has been no legal finding exactly on point, some evaluees decline to be interviewed out of fear of self-incrimination. Other evaluees believe, accurately or not, that if they provide the evaluator with as little information as possible, it will be more difficult to commit them.

Because psychological evaluations typically involve an interview, the evaluator must determine how comfortable she is reaching opinions without benefit of an interview. In addition, the evaluator should be prepared to justify this decision under cross-examination. In such cases, the evaluator is left to rely on records and collateral interview data. Even absent an interview, these sources can be used to reach opinions on the three psycholegal constructs of interest. In fact, as noted above, given the incentives for an evaluee to minimize a history of behavioral or sexual problems even if interviewed, relevant records and collateral interviews should weigh heavily in reaching opinions. Although performing an evaluation without conducting an interview is not ideal, it is ethical as long as the evaluator has made a reasonable effort to obtain one

BEWARE
Realize that an individual may rationally decide not to participate in an SVP interview if he were to conclude that such participation would make commitment more likely; moreover, the individual's attorney may so advise him.

INFO

The acceptable possibilities for interviewing SVP evaluees could be summarized as follows:

1. The evaluee elects to participate in the interview.

    ● This situation requires no special considerations by the evaluator.

2. The evaluee is offered an interview, shows an understanding of the nature of the interview, but declines to participate.

    ● The evaluator has proceeded properly and may continue the evaluation, based on use of information other than the interview.

    ● The evaluator should articulate any limitations on her opinion that she concludes are present due to the lack of an interview.

3. The evaluator offers the evaluee an interview but observes that the evaluee appears incompetent to consent to the interview.

    ● The evaluator should be aware before interviewing the evaluee what the specific jurisdiction's procedures are for dealing with individuals who are incompetent in SVP evaluations, typically because of psychosis.

(Committee on Ethical Guidelines for Forensic Psychologists, 1991, Principle, VI.H., p. 663). Whatever the disadvantages of the interview, they are outweighed by the opportunity to ask certain questions, follow up on certain answers, observe the individual, administer relevant testing, and score specialized measures. Nonetheless, interviews are not always possible, and the reader is referred to Chapter 2 for a review of the empirical referents from a file review that would provide evidence on the three psycholegal constructs in SVP cases.

5
chapter

Obtaining Collateral Information

It is unusual in SVP cases to interview past victims. SVP evaluations are typically done many years after the offense. When access to prior victims is limited or they are unavailable, such collateral interviews are impractical. In addition, there may well be ethical considerations in re-interviewing victims, who may be doing their best to put the prior trauma behind them. Instead, collateral information regarding victim and witness statements is typically obtained through a file review. In those rare cases in which a victim is accessible, in some states, for example Florida, the custom is for evaluators not to initiate direct contact with past victims. If and when past victims are to be contacted, that is done through the Office of the State Attorney (who will be representing the state), either directly by the assistant state attorney or by a victim's advocate.

Statements of prior victims and witnesses, when available, can provide useful information concerning the nature of the evaluee's offense characteristics. However, it is not unusual for an evaluee to plead guilty to only a small fraction of what was originally alleged or what the victim and witness statements indicate occurred. This presents a dilemma for the evaluator. Does the evaluator assume that what was originally alleged actually occurred? Is the evaluator limited to only the facts to which the evaluee pled guilty? We make some recommendations on this issue next.

The answers to these questions may vary from jurisdiction to jurisdiction and, at times, from one courtroom to another. The evaluator is not a legal fact-finder. Consequently, one option for the evaluator is to assume as accurate only the factual basis for the evaluee's guilty plea (or conviction by trial). This course will lead to a conservative approach to diagnosis and result in a more limited offense history. But it has the benefit of keeping the evaluator out of the role of finder of fact, an inappropriate role for an evaluator. This approach has the potential disadvantage of making a more limited finding, and perhaps an inaccurate finding, than would be possible if the evaluator were to consider the broader allegations sufficiently established to be admitted as factual. The holding of the SVP proceedings before a jury or before a judge and the nature of the burden and standard of proof may determine whether unproven allegations are considered factual by the court. The evaluator should be aware of what is considered acceptable and normative in his jurisdiction.

Another option is to give a range of findings, depending on what factual assumptions the court wishes to make. This approach leaves

determination of the facts where it belongs—with the court. It provides the court with guidance as to what opinions the evaluator would have depending on what facts are assumed. This approach has the advantage of providing the court with a range of opinions, each opinion tied to specific factual assumptions. For example, the evaluator could say to the court, "My opinion is A if one accepts that the four prior arrests for rape, even though none resulted in a conviction for a sexual offense, actually reflect four separate sexual offenses. My opinion is B if one accepts that these four prior arrests do not reflect any instances of sexual offending." (And perhaps iterations in between, if they affected the opinion as ultimately A or B.) This approach deconstructs the opinion so that the evaluator is discussing factors that can be clearly identified and acknowledges the areas about which the evaluator is uncertain. The benefits of such clarity are considerable. The disadvantage of this approach is that it does not lead to a single, firm opinion (with the usual term of art, a reasonable degree of professional certainty) regarding the core psycholegal issues. Some evaluators feel compelled (correctly or not) to offer a final opinion, and some jurisdictions may require such an opinion. However, this problem is simply one version of the ultimate issue question, and there is something very appealing about being as precise as possible about what one knows and does not know.

5
chapter

Psychological Testing

In performing mental health evaluations, forensic psychologists historically have administered broad-brush psychological tests, which assess a range of general personality characteristics. Although an SVP evaluator may wish to perform psychological testing to derive broad information about personality or cognitive functioning, at present, no data exist that would relate traditional psychological test results to the specific psycholegal questions relevant in SVP commitment cases— that is, mental abnormality (as defined in these cases), volitional impairment, or increased risk. Nonetheless, personality tests may have use in SVP cases, as long as the evaluator does not expect too much from the tests or draw conclusions that lack an empirical foundation.

With regard to potential uses of psychological testing, we propose the following:

- *Assessment of mental disorder.* In SVP cases, mental disorder is broadly defined, as noted earlier. There is an extensive literature on the use of objective personality tests, such as the Minnesota Multiphasic Personality Inventory-2 (MMPI-2; Butcher, Dahlstrom, Graham, Tellegen, & Kaemmer, 1989), Millon Clinical Multiaxial Inventory–III (MCMI-III; Millon, 1997), and the Personality Assessment Inventory (PAI; Morey, 1991) to assess mental disorders and classify prisoners in correctional populations generally (e.g., Edens, Cruise, Buffington-Vollum, 2001; Mullen & Edens, 2008; National Institute of Corrections, 2004). Consequently, results from such testing might inform (although not be synonymous with) an opinion about the presence of a mental disorder. The evaluator should not make a diagnosis based solely on psychological test data. These data are only a part of what the evaluator would consider in reaching a diagnosis or an opinion on the presence of a mental disorder.

- *Assessment of response style.* If the evaluators disregard or minimize consideration of the evaluee's self-report, then it is useful to say that one reason for doing so was the measured response style as reflected in a defensive presentation on the relevant scales of a standardized personality test. The above-noted instruments all include scales that assess response style and could be useful in this regard. Moreover, although minimization and denial are generally the rule in SVP cases, exaggeration of symptoms is not unheard of (see, for example, DeClue, 2002).

However, we caution the evaluator not to overreach in her conclusions. There are no studies that relate psychological test results to

SVP commitment status. Currently, there is no information on what psychological testing pattern or patterns might characterize individuals found suitable for SVP commitment. One should not expect any test to make this distinction. The use of a personality test is only to help assess mental disorder and response style, both of which are relevant in forming an opinion in an SVP case. Additionally, with regard to traditional self-report personality tests, it is possible that SVP evaluees would respond by minimizing psychological difficulties, given the incentive for them to be less than honest to avoid being committed. Although most of the major objective personality tests have validity scales, our experience is that a defensive response pattern is most common, resulting in a test protocol with limited usefulness (other than the information gained regarding the evaluee's response style itself).

Our recommendation regarding psychological testing is consistent with the position taken in the manual for California SVP evaluators:

> The use of psychological tests in SVP evaluations is left to the discretion of the clinical evaluator, but should be selected appropriately to answer the clinical referral questions. While some evaluators prefer to give a more extensive battery of tests, others may find that a thorough clinical interview and record review provides adequate basis to determine which offenders are at risk for future sexual reoffense by reason of their diagnosed mental disorder. (California Department of Mental Health, 2004, p. 21)

In cross-examination, questioning is far more likely to focus on whether the evaluee meets *DSM-IV-TR* criteria than on MMPI-2 responses. As noted earlier, antisocial personality disorder (or psychopathy) and the paraphilias are the most common diagnostic focus in SVP evaluations. General personality tests are not notably helpful in analyzing paraphilic interests. The most convincing demonstration of antisocial tendencies often comes from the respondent's history. The degree to which the evaluee is open and honest in interview responses can often best be assessed by comparing responses to records and other collateral

BEWARE Psychological testing can provide useful information on mental disorders and response style, but cannot distinguish patterns that make an individual suitable for SVP commitment.

5 chapter

information. Nonetheless, psychological testing may provide useful information, admittedly self-report, regarding the evaluee's symptoms and personality.

Psychophysiological Assessment

There is considerable debate among sex offender assessment professionals over psychophysiological assessment. Given the likelihood of minimization in a sex offender's self-report, researchers and clinicians specializing in sex offenders have for decades attempted to use psychophysiological measures of sexual deviance in an effort to obtain objective measures of such deviance. A person's pattern of sexual desires—what Money (1986) has called a "lovemap"—is, for the most part, not readily apparent to others. Physiological signs such as penile tumescence or vaginal lubrication may be considered to be indicators of sexual arousal. Over several decades, sexologists have attempted to develop a standardized method of measuring psychophysiological responses to sexual stimuli. Although the attempt to obtain an objective measure of deviant sexual interest is reasonable, particularly when self-report is inaccurate, there are problems with the commonly used psychophysiological measures that presently limit their use in SVP evaluations.

Phallometry

The psychophysiological assessment method with the longest research history is penile plethysmography, or phallometry. The most common method involves measuring the circumference of the individual's penis while he watches or listens to a variety of sexual stimuli. Decades ago, Abel and his colleagues documented deviant sexual arousal patterns among sex offenders using phallometry (see, for example, Abel, Becker, Murphy, & Flanagan, 1981). Numerous studies since have found that at least some (but not all) sex offenders have deviant sexual arousal patterns when assessed by phallometry (see Fabian, 2005, pp. 136–138). A widely cited meta-analysis by Hanson and Bussiere (1998) found sexual deviance as assessed by the plethysmograph to be a relatively

BEWARE
Commonly used psychophysiological measures have limited use in SVP evaluations.

good correlate of sex offender recidivism for child molesters but not for rapists. The practice guidelines of the Association for the Treatment of Sexual Abusers (2005, p. 16) also indicate that phallometry is a useful method of "corroborating client self-report."

Although phallometry has merit, it is the most intrusive of the psychophysiologic assessment procedures, as the individual must place a sensor around his penis and view or listen to sexual

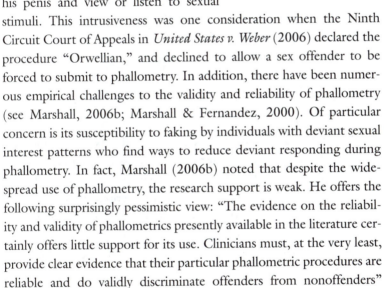

INFO

The Screening Scale for
Pedophilic Interests
(SSPI) has four criteria:

1.   Male victim

2.   More than one victim

3.   Victim aged 11 or younger

4.   Unrelated victim

stimuli. This intrusiveness was one consideration when the Ninth Circuit Court of Appeals in *United States v. Weber* (2006) declared the procedure "Orwellian," and declined to allow a sex offender to be forced to submit to phallometry. In addition, there have been numerous empirical challenges to the validity and reliability of phallometry (see Marshall, 2006b; Marshall & Fernandez, 2000). Of particular concern is its susceptibility to faking by individuals with deviant sexual interest patterns who find ways to reduce deviant responding during phallometry. In fact, Marshall (2006b) noted that despite the widespread use of phallometry, the research support is weak. He offers the following surprisingly pessimistic view: "The evidence on the reliability and validity of phallometrics presently available in the literature certainly offers little support for its use. Clinicians must, at the very least, provide clear evidence that their particular phallometric procedures are reliable and do validly discriminate offenders from nonoffenders" (2006b, p. 12).

The evaluator may consider using a proxy for phallometry. For example, Seto and Lalumière (2001), using a sample of over 1,000 individuals, developed a brief screening scale to identify pedophilic interests among child molesters. Their resultant scale, the Screening Scale for Pedophilic Interests (SSPI), showed a significant statistical relationship to phallometric results, as well as reasonable sensitivity and specificity in discriminating pedophilic child molesters from the nonpedophilic. However, the evaluator should be aware that the SSPI is, as indicated in its title, a screening scale. Although it can indicate a direction for further inquiry and assessment, it should not be used by itself, any more than should phallometry, to reach a diagnosis of paraphilia.

Polygraphy

A second psychophysiological assessment method sometimes used in evaluating sex offenders is polygraphy, commonly referred to as lie detection. Recent surveys have found polygraphy increasingly recommended as a standard for monitoring sex offenders (Branaman & Gallagher, 2005). As the ATSA guidelines (Association for the Treatment of Sexual Abusers, 2005, p. 43) indicate, "Post conviction sex offender polygraph testing is a specialized form of general polygraph testing that has come into widespread use in the United States." The ATSA guidelines (2005, p. 43) suggest that polygraphy is designed to serve two purposes:

1. generate information beyond what can be obtained from other self-report measures, and

2. increase compliance with supervision conditions and treatment procedures.

Polygraphy is believed by some sex offender experts to increase the level of offense acknowledgement among sex offenders. In fact, some sex offender treatment providers have recommended that convicted sex offenders be required to submit to periodic polygraph testing as a condition of probation. Some states have also incorporated this into the standard conditions of "sex offender probation." Some commentators have recommended that polygraphy be used in SVP commitment cases to assess the nature of deviant sexual urges and fantasies. For example, Fabian (2005, pp. 145–146) states:

> In addition to phallometric data, this author recommends the use of polygraph testing to assess the veracity of the offender's self-reports, especially those relating to an offender's current sexual fantasies. Polygraphs can offer valuable data relevant to current sexual fantasies, masturbatory practices, and past sexual offenses or behaviors.

However, at present, the reliability and validity data for polygraphy do not support its use in SVP evaluations. In a recent review, Branaman and Gallagher (2005) note that empirical studies indicate a significant risk of false positive errors. Moreover, although the level

BEWARE Current data do not support the use of the polygraph in SVP evaluations.

of false positives may be acceptable when polygraph questions deal only with the instant offense (or at least this may be so in controlled research studies), sex offender polygraphs are frequently broader in focus than a specific incident, including questions on deviant sexual fantasies and intent. False positive rates are higher when the questions are broadened in this manner (Branaman & Gallagher, 2005), presenting a substantial risk of error. These conclusions parallel those of the National Research Council (2002), which reviewed the literature on use of polygraphs in employment settings and raised concerns of whether its use should be limited to investigations of specific incidents, where its error rate was lowest. In addition, the use of a polygraph in an SVP evaluation raises the possibility that the results of an entire evaluation might be excluded on the basis of use of a single measure—the polygraph—that has been held inadmissible since *Frye* was decided in 1923.

Viewing Time

A third psychophysiological assessment method that is sometimes used for assessing sex offenders is viewing time, that is, unobtrusively measuring the amount of time an individual looks at visual stimuli. The assumption is that an individual will spend more time looking at visual stimuli he finds more sexually interesting. The primary method for assessing viewing time is a proprietary procedure referred to as the Abel Assessment for Sexual Interest (AASI; Abel, Huffman, Warberg, & Holland, 1998; Abel, Jordan, Hand, Holland, & Phipps, 2001).

However, there is considerable debate in the literature over the accuracy of the AASI, with findings outside of Abel's laboratory indicating relatively poor classification accuracy (e.g., Fischer & Smith, 1999; Smith & Fischer, 1999). Moreover, there are serious questions about the admissibility of the AASI. In a widely discussed opinion, *Ready v. Commonwealth* (2005), the Massachusetts Court of Appeals found that the AASI did not meet *Daubert* standards of admissibility. In a highly critical opinion, the *Ready* court opined that the AASI lacked empirical validity, that it was not generally accepted, and that it had an unacceptably high error rate. Although the *Ready* decision

BEWARE
The admissibility of AASI results is in question.

is not binding on other jurisdictions, it suggests skepticism in the legal community about the usefulness and admissibility of the AASI.

Specialized Risk Assessment Tools

The area in which perhaps the greatest progress has been made in recent decades is in the actuarial assessment of risk. Criteria on these instruments are selected on the basis of their actuarial relationship with sex offender recidivism in populations of known recidivists, usually through a meta-analysis, which combines a number of prior studies. A variety of actuarial risk assessment tools are used in evaluating SVP cases, including the Sex Offender Risk Appraisal Guide (SORAG; Quinsey, Harris, et al., 1998); the Rapid Risk Assessment for Sex Offence Recidivism (RRASOR; Hanson, 1997), and Static-99 (Hanson & Thornton, 1999, 2000). The Static-99 is, anecdotally, perhaps the most widely used of these. Actuarial risk assessment tools focus heavily on static, historical risk factors. Briefly, the characteristics of actuarial risk assessment tools are as follows:

- *Sex Offender Risk Appraisal Guide (SORAG):* This is a 14-factor risk assessment instrument that includes historical variables, as well as administration of the Hare Psychopathy Checklist-Revised and assessment of sexual deviance as assessed through phallometry. It necessitates collection of accurate historical data, but can be completed without substantial cooperation by the offender (other than the phallometry aspect). It is designed to assess the probability that a sex offender is apt to recidivate.

- *Rapid Risk Assessment for Sex Offense Recidivism:* This is a brief actuarial scale created from four variables found through meta-analysis to independently predict recidivism among sex offenders. These include prior sexual arrests (most heavily weighted), age, targeting of male victims, and whether any victims were unrelated to the offender.

- *Static-99:* This instrument combines items from the RRASOR and an additional instrument, the SACJ-Min. Studies thus far indicate that its predictive accuracy exceeds that of either of the previous instruments used alone. It is based completely on static variables including prior sex offenses, unrelated victims, stranger victims, male victims, age, never having married, noncontact sex offenses, prior sentences, current nonsexual violence, and prior nonsexual violence. It is designed to measure long-term risk potential.

Table 5.1 | Use of Actuarial Tools

Advantages	Disadvantages
• Criteria selected on the basis of empirical relationship to recidivism	• Typically do not include dynamic risk factors, meaning they do not identify treatment targets or reflect changes over time
• Widely admitted as evidence in SVP hearings	• May exclude relevant areas if those areas were not sampled in validating meta-analyses
• Anecdotal (and limited empirical) evidence indicates most widely used risk assessment method in SVP hearings	• Rigid scoring and narrow scope may disengage evaluator from evaluation process
• Some, such as Static-99, are straightforward to score	• Ignores context and situation
• Most can be scored from archival data	• May not capture important information in unusual cases (e.g., the rare individual who commits sexual offenses as a result of a psychotic disorder or one whose offenses stem from significant intellectual deficits)

5
chapter

Although actuarial risk tools are widely used (and widely admitted as evidence), structured professional judgment tools, such as the previously discussed SVR-20, are an empirically supported alternative. Structured professional judgment tools are constructed by an analysis of the existing empirical and theoretical literature. As part of the development and validation process, the structured professional judgment tool can be subjected to validity studies, both concurrent and predictive, to determine its ability to predict recidivism.

We offer no prescription regarding which of the two approaches to take. Indeed, the two approaches are not mutually exclusive. The evaluator should consider the advantages and disadvantages of each approach and proceed accordingly. As Boer (2006) noted, there is continuing debate over which approach is better.

The advantages and disadvantages of the respective approaches are listed in Tables 5.1 and 5.2.

Table 5.2 | Use of Structured Professional Judgment

Advantages	Disadvantages
• Based on rational analysis of the empirical literature	• Anecdotal evidence indicates not as widely used or accepted by evaluators in SVP cases
• Many instruments include dynamic risk factors and are more comprehensive in scope than actuarial instruments	• Specific criterion may not have supported empirical relationship with recidivism
• Due to comprehensiveness, can be used as an organizational tool for the report	• Allows more room for error by a user not familiar with the underlying empirical literature
• Predictive ability in validation studies as good as actuarial instruments	• May not be applicable to populations not included in the instrument development (e.g., female offenders)

Summary

In this chapter, we have discussed the general sequence of SVP evaluations and evaluator considerations at each stage of the sequence. Typically, the evaluator first reviews the file to orient himself to the case. In SVP cases, a thorough file review is critical, given that the evaluee's history is frequently a major factor in determining whether to recommend an SVP commitment, and much of that history is documented in the frequently voluminous file. Next in the sequence is an interview of the evaluee. We have discussed considerations regarding the not-uncommon circumstance of an evaluee's declining to participate in an interview. We suggested some reasons why formal psychological testing can be useful, even if testing does not directly address the psycholegal questions at hand. We then recommended against use of physiological assessment methods, for a variety of reasons detailed in this chapter. Finally, we reviewed the issues associated with specialized risk assessment tools that are commonly used in SVP assessments.

Interpretation | 6

Overview

By now, the evaluator will have reviewed the file, interviewed the evaluee (if the evaluee was willing), and possibly performed psychological and specialized testing. In some cases, the evaluator may have even interviewed a collateral source to clarify a particular point. Although in many forensic cases the evaluator does the usual array of collateral interviews (family, friends, employers, teachers), this would be unusual in an SVP evaluation. SVP evaluees have typically been incarcerated for many years prior to the beginning of an SVP proceeding. Consequently, any information from the usual collaterals (such as family or friends) would be both dated and based on distant recollection; most collateral contacts are contemporary (or at least recent) sources of information, such as a probation or parole officer or institutional staff. If the file on the evaluee is extensive and the interview(s) long, as is frequently true in SVP cases, the evaluator now has a large amount of data to organize and interpret. It is the evaluator's job to describe how the information she has obtained relates to the psycholegal questions before the court. In some states, a state agency may be an intermediate consumer of the report, and the report may need to be prepared in a way that is satisfactory to that state agency. Nonetheless, the court is the ultimate consumer.

The court is not interested in every aspect of the evaluee's life. Rather, the court—whether in a jury trial or a bench trial—needs to make a single determination: Is the evaluee committable under that jurisdiction's SVP statute? To make this decision, the court will focus on the three interrelated psycholegal constructs: mental abnormality, volitional impairment, and risk. The evaluator will want

to organize the information about the evaluee and provide interpretations in these three domains. It is not good practice to make the report like an embedded-figures test, placing the interpretations in a maze of correct but irrelevant information. Interpretations should be limited to these three issues and information should be tailored to focus on them, because they are the issues before the court.

Jurisdiction Considerations

There may be case law or statutes in the evaluator's jurisdiction that will lead the evaluator to tailor interpretations to fit the specific parameters of the jurisdiction. Some jurisdictions, for example, have case law that provides guidance on what factors are relevant for different aspects of the three psycholegal issues, such as volitional impairment. (The interested reader should consult Mercado, Schopp, and Bornstein [2005], discussed earlier, for some examples of case law in this area.) The more closely an evaluator's interpretations conform to what is legally relevant and permissible in that jurisdiction, the more credence the evaluator's interpretations and opinions are likely to receive.

In addition, in offering interpretations concerning the three psycholegal constructs, there may well be informal norms among other experienced evaluators in the relevant jurisdiction. Experienced local evaluators will have testified before the judges hearing these cases and, in many cases, been cross-examined by prosecutors and defense attorneys who specialize in these cases. As a result, experienced local evaluators know the formal and informal rules regarding admissibility and relevance, as well as a particular court's style and preference. For example, in some jurisdictions, the court may expect at the outset of testimony a complete description of the documents the evaluator has reviewed as well as all other sources of information. In other jurisdictions, in the interest of time, the court will prefer to rely on the sources of information listed in the report itself. In certain jurisdictions, the court will want an ultimate opinion (i.e., whether the

evaluator concludes that the evaluee meets the standards for SVP commitment), whereas in other jurisdictions, the court would consider such an ultimate opinion improper. In some jurisdictions, the court may expect an opinion on volitional impairment; in others, the court would prefer a list of factors that bear on volitional impairment, with an overall determination of the level of volitional impairment left to the court.

BEWARE
Empirical research is limited in some areas, such as volitional impairment. When an opinion is required, follow the case law in the relevant jurisdiction.

Using Data to Form Opinions

The evaluator should systematically review the data to form a foundation for his opinions. The evaluator should indicate the psycholegal issue(s) for which particular data are relevant. Ideally, the data upon which the evaluator relies most heavily should have an established empirical relationship with the psycholegal issue at hand. When this empirical foundation is lacking, there should be a legally established relationship between the information and the psycholegal question (e.g., case law on the admissibility or relevance of that information). For example, there is little empirical foundation for an opinion on volitional impairment. Nonetheless, an opinion on this issue is required in some jurisdictions, and the evaluator can obtain some guidance by reviewing case law findings on the issue. We have reservations, however, about offering an opinion for which there is little empirical support. The evaluator should carefully consider whether an expectation that he offer an opinion on volitional impairment goes beyond what one can reliably offer as an expert and, at a minimum, acknowledge the lack of agreement within the field on this issue.

Evaluating Hypotheses

The evaluator should make the basis for an opinion as transparent as possible. One way to do this is to use the data to generate hypotheses, or potential explanations, regarding the three prongs of the SVP civil commitment proceeding. For each hypothesis, the evaluator can describe the data underlying it, as well as the inferences that lead to that hypothesis. Each hypothesis can then be evaluated as to how well it fits the available data and guiding theory.

6
chapter

The following vignette provides an example of how one might begin to evaluate competing hypotheses.

> First, the illegal sexual activity could be a reflection of a broadly antisocial personality and lifestyle in which the individual violates a variety of societal norms and laws. If this were the case, one would expect to see the usual indicators of an antisocial personality disorder, such as prior criminal offenses (including nonsexual offenses), substance abuse, and both job and relationship instability. There is no evidence of this with Mr. Smith. He shows no juvenile history of delinquent activity and no juvenile association with delinquent peers. As an adult, he has a stable work and relationship history. Consequently, it is my opinion that I can rule out this possible explanation.
>
> Second, the illegal sexual activity could be a reflection of a pedophilic sexual preference. If this explanation were to apply, one would expect to see significant evidence of preferential interest in sexual activity with minors, including perhaps an extensive collection of child pornography (to the exclusion of adult pornography), and both frequent and chronic sex offenses against children. In Mr. Smith's case, he frequently explored chat rooms focusing on sexual activity with minors. In addition, he has viewed child pornography online, and when his hard drive was forensically analyzed, over 2,000 images and videos of child pornography were found. He was involved in using peer-to-peer software to trade child pornographic images over the Internet, leading to a past charge for distribution of child pornography. In Mr. Smith's most recent offense, he not only chatted online with the young girl about having sexual activity, but also arranged to have the girl's underage female friend meet him for sexual activity. His history of sexual activity with young girls stretches back almost two decades prior to his most recent incarceration. Finally, he has a limited history of adult sexual relationships. Consequently, there is substantial evidence indicating that he is a preferential pedophile.

BEST PRACTICE
In anticipation of cross-examination, systematically consider evidence for alternative explanations.

This vignette illustrates a few points. First, the implicit predictions for each hypothesis are

BEST PRACTICE

Be aware of the literature on which the hypothesis is based and be prepared to explain that literature in court if necessary.

articulated clearly at the outset. For example, with regard to the first hypothesis—that is, that the sex offenses were due to a broadly antisocial orientation—the evaluator first needs to consider what one would expect to see if that hypothesis were applicable. These expectations would be based on the empirical and theoretical literature on this topic.

Once the evaluator considers what would be expected if the hypothesis were valid, the evaluator then considers the information on the evaluee to determine whether that information provides a good fit with that hypothesis. The previous vignette was intentionally constructed to clearly illustrate this fit. In actual practice, however, the fit may not be so obvious.

Unclear Fit between Data and Hypothesis

There are two reasons why it may be unclear whether the data in an SVP case fit an hypothesis. First, there may be a firm and comprehensive set of facts (facts broadly construed, including interview, records review, and testing data), but the pattern of facts does not neatly conform to a specific hypothesis. For instance, in an SVP case, there may be clear indications in the records and the history of antisocial behavior and sexually deviant behavior, but they are neither severe nor chronic enough to lead to a diagnosis of either antisocial personality disorder or a paraphilia. Consequently, it may not be possible to determine whether the evaluee's illegal sexual behavior in that case resulted from primarily antisocial factors, deviant sexual interest, or some combination of the two, and it may be unclear whether the evaluee's history warrants a *DSM* diagnosis.

Second, the facts themselves may be uncertain. It is not at all infrequent that in the voluminous files available in these cases, conflicting information appears regarding the evaluee's history. Moreover, there may have been numerous allegations that, if taken as factual, establish a pattern—such as that of antisocial or paraphilic behavior (or both). However, if these allegations were not part of the factual basis of the evaluee's guilty plea or trial conviction, it is unclear

6
chapter

whether they can be considered as factual for the purposes of the SVP evaluation. This may depend on the case law or applicable evidentiary law in the jurisdiction. Consequently, the evaluator may not know what facts to use in testing hypotheses.

Offering Conditional Opinions

The evaluator has a few options in these circumstances, and there are advantages and disadvantages to each. One option is for the evaluator to provide conditional conclusions. That is, the evaluator can acknowledge either the contradictory or uncertain evidence in the case, and indicate that the conclusions regarding the relevant SVP issues would depend on the assumptions made about these underlying facts. The evaluator could then allow the court (or jury, depending on the jurisdiction) to make a determination on the underlying facts. This would allow the evaluator to indicate to which hypothesis, or explanation, these now-established facts best conform. This option is the safest in some respects, allowing the court to assume its proper role as finder of fact and not placing the evaluator in this role. However, some courts expect the evaluator to reach a conclusion on the components of SVP commitment, so offering a conditional opinion may be unacceptable in such a jurisdiction. As we have noted previously, it may simply not be realistic for a court to expect an expert to offer an opinion, especially an ultimate opinion, in some cases. One might say, in such a jurisdiction, either a) available evidence shows that he does meet criteria or b) available evidence does not clearly show that he meets criteria (DeClue, G. personal communication, December 8, 2006). As we discussed in Chapter 5, it is quite reasonable to sometimes opine that "it depends on whether A, B, or C is accurate and factual."

It is not unusual for an evaluee to deny having committed the offense, even if in the past he pled guilty to having done so. Consequently, the evaluator should have a conceptual strategy for dealing with the possibility that the evaluee will deny all or part of what has been alleged or even to that which he has pled guilty. Conditional conclusions, contingent upon which facts are assumed, are quite reasonable under such circumstances. Given that the evaluator is not a fact-finder and the evaluator's opinion may well depend on the facts, it is up to the court to determine which facts to assume. If one's opinion were presented in this manner, it would be difficult for the court to demand that the evaluator make an ultimate conclusion. Of course, a judge or attorney might find such testimony irritating and prefer a more conclusory approach, but we would hope that is not a major consideration in determining what testimony is appropriate.

Reaching Conclusions

A second option is to reach a conclusion regarding the hypotheses that are best explained by the facts, as incomplete or conflicting as those facts may be. One could place less weight on facts that are in dispute, or one could simply assume that such facts are established, deferring to the court on any final finding of fact. The evaluator should be clear about the extent to which she is relying on disputed facts. This approach has some justification. In traditional civil commitment cases (that is, those not involving convicted sex offenders), evaluators routinely make diagnoses and form opinions about dangerousness to self and others without any prior judicial findings of fact. Many persons civilly committed under those circumstances may have no history of criminal charges, much less convictions. Yet, in those cases, evaluators routinely review the file, draw conclusions about risk, make diagnoses, and form opinions on civil commitment. In the end, it is up to the court to determine whether the facts upon which the evaluator is basing an opinion are admissible and reliable.

In jurisdictions where it is expected that the evaluator will reach a conclusion on the three SVP psycholegal issues, this alternative may be reasonable. If an SVP evaluator is taking this approach, the factual assumptions should be made clear. The court, if it chooses, can reach other factual conclusions, and the evaluator could, at that point, indicate how other inferences and conclusions would flow from those changed factual assumptions.

Formulating Opinions Related to SVP Commitment

Formulating an opinion in an SVP case involves gathering evidence to confirm or disconfirm the presence of the three interrelated psycholegal constructs of mental abnormality, volitional impairment, and elevated risk. Heilbrun, Marczyk, and DeMatteo (2002) recommend a three-stage procedure for translating legal constructs into mental health constructs. They suggest the following:

- First, identify the relevant legal construct, by reviewing the relevant statutory and case law, as well as legal scholarship on the topic.

- Second, operationalize the legal constructs. That is, determine how these constructs can be measured and what methods might be used to measure them.

- Third, gather information in the relevant domains to assess these constructs.

To the above three steps we would add a fourth step: Use the information gathered to form and test hypotheses on the fit of the facts to the legal constructs.

The SVP evaluator should follow a similar process in determining how to proceed in his jurisdiction (see Fig. 6.1). First, the evaluator should understand the legal constructs by reviewing relevant statutes and case law. Such materials are readily accessible over the Internet, a law library (for example, in the local courthouse), or from attorneys who specialize in SVP cases in the evaluator's jurisdiction. Second, the evaluator should determine the mental health constructs that best approximate the relevant legal constructs. This can be done by reviewing the scholarly literature on the subject and by consulting with colleagues who perform similar work. The evaluator should determine the optimal approach to gathering information to assess the mental health constructs found to best approximate the relevant legal constructs. Sources would include the scholarly literature that

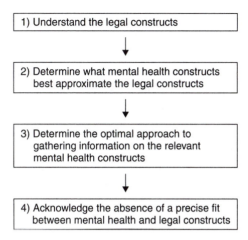

Figure 6.1 Steps to Formulating an Opinion

has developed regarding the instruments and procedures best suited for SVP evaluations and whether they have been subjected to a *Frye* or *Daubert* challenge in that particular jurisdiction. Additionally, it is frequently helpful to consult with colleagues who perform these evaluations in one's state to seek their views on the empirical referents that are most suitable to capture the three interrelated legal constructs of interest. A new evaluator might learn from attending training workshops and should be aware of statements by various professional organizations (e.g., the American Psychological Association, the American Psychiatric Association, the Association for the Treatment of Sexual Abusers, the American Bar Association). Evaluators should be knowledgeable about forensic mental health assessment, risk assessment, sexuality, and deviant sexuality. Finally, the evaluator should acknowledge the absence of a precise fit between mental health and legal constructs.

Formulating an Opinion Regarding Mental Abnormality

The first element in an SVP evaluation is the presence of a mental abnormality. Hence, the evaluator must generate and review data relevant to a potential *DSM* diagnosis. With regard to Axis I diagnoses, a paraphilia is the most common diagnosis, typically pedophilia or paraphilia NOS.

On occasion, during the interview the evaluee himself will provide a significant history of sexual deviance, making a paraphilia diagnosis straightforward. However, given the incentives for the evaluee to minimize such a history, revelations during the interview of illegal sexual behavior are unusual. No specific diagnosis is required by law (indeed, no diagnosis of any kind is required by law). There may well be findings of a mental disorder that falls outside the *DSM*—psychopathy is a good example. Use of the *DSM* is simply one means of ensuring a systematic approach to collecting and organizing this information, but other kinds of behavioral and symptomatic information would be relevant as well.

Paraphilia

It is likely that the evaluator will need to rely heavily on information other than the evaluee's self-report in reaching a paraphilia diagnosis. The evaluator is interested in chronicity, frequency, and severity of paraphilic behavior in the evaluee's history. In particular, prior charges and convictions for sex offenses provide a foundation for inferences in this area. In addition, in some cases the file will include victim and witness accounts, which allow a fuller picture of the nature of the evaluee's illegal sexual behavior (at least as alleged). Given the frequent lack of an accurate self-report, the evaluee's documented history of illegal sexual behavior may provide an excellent indicator of the extent to which he has a paraphilia.

It is not possible from a file review to obtain direct evidence of internal psychological states, such as sexually arousing urges or fantasies, unless the evaluee has previously made statements about such fantasies. These must be inferred from documented events in the file. In

BEST PRACTICE

Consider the specific *DSM-IV-TR* criteria for a paraphilia when formulating an opinion. These are as follows:

1. Intense sexually arousing fantasies, sexual urges, or behaviors involving

2. nonhuman objects, the suffering or humiliation of one's partner or children, or other non-consenting persons

3. that occur over a period of at least 6 months, and

4. these urges, fantasies, or behavior cause the individual marked distress or functional impairment. (American Psychiatric Association, 2000, p. 566)

Chapters 2 and 5, we discussed some potential indicators of a paraphilia, including obvious signs of sexual arousal reported in the offenses (e.g., ejaculation), high frequency and chronicity of sex offending, and committing illegal sexual acts despite a significant likelihood of being caught. The evaluator should be alert to additional historical indicators consistent with a paraphilia, such as collections of sexually deviant pornography (e.g., child or

INFO

The criteria for the RRASOR are the following:

1. Prior sex offenses
2. Age at release
3. Victim gender
4. Relationship to victim

sadistic pornography) that are consistent with the offense pattern. All these indicators support an interpretation of criteria 1–3 of paraphilia. Incarceration itself supports the functional impairment criterion.

The evaluator should also recall from Chapter 5 the Screening Scale for Pedophilic Interests (SSPI), developed by Seto and Lalumiére (2001), consisting of male victim; more than one victim; victim aged 11 or younger; and unrelated victim. The SSPI has a distinct similarity to an accepted and empirically validated risk assessment scale, the Rapid Risk Assessment for Sexual Recidivism (RRASOR: Hanson, 1997).

This information, if present in the file, may assist in formulating an empirically grounded opinion regarding the presence of a paraphilia. However, we are not aware of cases in which the question of whether the SSPI meets *Daubert* or *Frye* standards has been addressed.

Consider the following vignette, illustrating how information in a hypothetical case might be organized to address the question of an Axis I paraphilia.

> Deviant interests are reflected in Mr. M.'s selection of young children, under age 12, which is associated with relatively higher risk for sexual recidivism. Records indicate that he took pleasure in offending against young children, pleasure that increased when the children screamed. All his victims were strangers, a factor that research suggests elevates his risk for recidivism. This offender has been known to have young male victims, and those who offend against young male victims are at higher risk for sexual recidivism than other groups of offenders. In addition, his sexual offending against

BEWARE Although the SSPI may be useful in generally guiding your thinking on the presence of a paraphilia, rely on more generally accepted specialized risk assessment tools to structure your opinions.

young children had an early onset, approximately age 15. All these factors indicate that Mr. M. has a mental abnormality, specifically a paraphilia. Many of the above factors are consistent with a diagnosis of pedophilia, as well as some elements consistent with *sexual sadism.*

In Mr. M.'s case, there is no evidence that would support the potentially competing hypothesis of his illegal sexual activity being directed by an antisocial or psychopathic personality style. His criminal history is limited to sex offending. He has no history of nonsexual crimes, violent or otherwise. He has no history of the impulsive, unstable lifestyle that typically indicates an antisocial personality. The serious legal and behavioral problems in Mr. M's life are associated only with his illegal sexual behavior.

As noted previously, because sex offenders generally and SVP evaluees particularly have so much incentive to minimize the extent of the sexual deviation in their history, evaluators for decades have sought physiological measures of the extent of sexual deviance. The two most common measures are phallometry and viewing-time measures. As discussed in Chapter 5, we do not recommend relying on either of these measures in SVP cases. Despite the popularity of these measures, there are empirical controversies with each (see Fischer & Smith, 1999; Marshall, 2006b; Smith & Fischer, 1999). There are also indications that courts are becoming skeptical of both measures (see *Ready v. Commonwealth*, 2005; *United States v. Weber*, 2006). Although there may be benefits to using these measures in other contexts, such as monitoring outpatient compliance, we recommend against their use in SVP commitment evaluations.

Antisocial Personality Disorder

After considering the data relevant to an Axis I disorder, the evaluator reviews the data bearing on an Axis II disorder. By definition, Axis II disorders are chronic conditions, so any Axis II diagnosis should be supported by materials from

BEWARE Physiological measures, such as phallometry and viewing time, are not recommended for use in SVP commitment evaluations.

the file reflecting a history of functional impairment prior to and sometimes during incarceration. Although any Axis II disorder is possible, in
SVP cases, the most common diagnosis is antisocial personality disorder
(APD). A thorough interview, perhaps using a structured or semistructured guide, is helpful; however, the problem of obtaining accurate self-
report remains. Therefore, a file review frequently provides the most
comprehensive information from which inferences can be drawn. The
evaluator can look for evidence that confirms (or disconfirms) that the
evaluee has APD (or its extreme variant, psychopathic personality).

The *DSM* diagnosis of APD refers to disregard for the rights of
others as reflected primarily in behaviors, or at least to constructs that
should be readily evident in behaviors. For instance, the *DSM* refers
to fights or assaults, to failure to sustain consistent work behavior, and
to acts that are grounds for arrests. Historical information indicating
whether these criteria are met can be reflected in work records, mar-
ital history records, and prior criminal history records. These areas are
typically summarized in pre-sentence investigation reports, and more
elaborate information may also be available. These *DSM-IV-TR* APD
criteria are similar to those reflected in what is called Factor 2 of
psychopathy—that is, chronic antisocial behavior.

A few of the *DSM-IV-TR* APD criteria focus on personality
attributes, and all of psychopathy Factor 1 focuses on a callous,
exploitive personality style. These attributes are more difficult to infer
from the file. At times, a thorough interview will reveal evidence of
this aspect of the evaluee. The *DSM-IV-TR* criterion of lack of
remorse may be apparent through an interview. The PCL-R criteria
of lack of empathy, lack of remorse, grandiosity, glibness, and lack of
realistic plans may also be apparent in an interview. For these personality criteria, reports on institutional adjustment may be helpful, particularly if the evaluee is in treatment. Treatment providers have
ongoing contact with the evaluee and have the opportunity to
observe the evaluee relating to peers. Consequently, treatment
reports can provide the evaluator with useful
information about the evaluee's interpersonal
style. Similarly, institutional work and housing
reports (as well as the evaluee's history of institutional disciplinary charges) can provide other

**BEST
PRACTICE**
Do a thorough file review to
gather evidence for antisocial
personality disorder.

indicators of the evaluee's ability to follow rules and relate to others respectfully.

Formulating an Opinion on Volitional Impairment

As previously discussed, there is perhaps no more controversial aspect to SVP evaluations than the opinion on volitional impairment. Whether to offer an opinion on the presence of volitional impairment has been hotly debated in the field. There are two positions the evaluator can take regarding offering an opinion on volitional impairment.

Objections to Offering an Opinion

The evaluator can take a conservative position, offering no opinion on volitional impairment. This position has the advantage of support among some commentators, who have found the construct of volitional impairment to be confused and unscientific (see Chapter 2). The typical objections to offering an opinion on volitional impairment include the following:

- There is no reliable way of distinguishing an inability to resist an urge from choosing to act on that urge.

- There is no statutory law guidance (or U.S. Supreme Court guidance in either *Hendricks* or *Crane*) on how that construct is to be defined or articulated.

- There is a lack of empirical research on the correlates of volitional impairment.

- Self-report may be an unreliable means of determining volitional impairment, particularly within this population.

- Given the controversy about the construct of volitional impairment, if there is any construct on which to avoid giving an opinion, it is this one.

Offering an Opinion

Despite these reservations, the evaluator may choose to offer an opinion on volitional impairment. This may in fact be expected in some jurisdictions—those in which the court would like an opinion (with "a reasonable degree of professional certainty") on whether the evaluee is civilly committable under the jurisdiction's SVP statute. Such an ultimate opinion would normally require views on the penultimate constructs that underlie that opinion, one of which is volitional impairment. Evaluators who choose not to give an opinion on volitional impairment may find their testimony discounted and their use limited before such courts. As we have argued, an evaluator must determine whether the jurisdiction's expectations for an opinion are within the reasonable and supportable limits of what the evaluator can offer. It may be the case that the evaluator will need to inform the court that the current state of the science does not permit an opinion on volitional impairment. If the evaluator does decide to offer an opinion on volitional impairment, he should inform the court of the limits of and the basis for the opinion. For example, consider the following hypothetical report excerpt:

> I concluded that the evaluee showed serious impairment in his ability to control his sexual urges, based solely on his continued aberrant behavior in the face of severe consequences. In this case, the evaluee continued to sexually abuse young boys over a period of 5 years. He did so despite repeated negative consequences, in particular multiple arrests with escalating legal consequences over this period. Moreover, he continued to relapse despite what he reported as strenuous efforts not to reoffend. In fact, the evaluee committed his last sex offense while on sex offender probation and involved in sex offender–specific treatment.

Awareness of and careful attention to the psychological and case law literature in this area (reviewed in Chapter 2) are helpful. The jurisdiction-specific case law can be particularly valuable in providing guidance on the parameters most relevant to the court. Although the evaluator is not expected to be an attorney, awareness of the case law context can aid the evaluator in determining what aspects of the individual are most relevant to the court. As Conroy and Murrie suggest,

BEST PRACTICE

If offering an opinion on volitional impairment, inform the court of the limits and basis of the opinion. Be guided by case law in this area, particularly in the relevant jurisdiction.

6
chapter

A first step, then, for professionals planning to conduct an SVP risk assessment is to make certain they have *current* knowledge of the statutes, case law, and rules in the jurisdiction in which the evaluation will be done. The legal landscape is ever shifting; new laws are passed and new case law is decided. (2007, p. 183) [italics in original].

Organizing the Relevant Materials

Other than having the evaluee state that he found himself unable to control strong, deviant, sexual urges (which, in our experience, rarely occurs), the information relevant to volitional impairment comes primarily from the historical file materials. The evaluator may wish to organize the materials along the following two lines, per Doren's (2002) suggestion:

- Historical events that indicate an Axis I cause of volitional impairment (through strong deviant sexual urges overwhelming the evaluee's controls, thus causing him to have a limited view of his choices)

- Historical events that indicate an Axis II cause of volitional impairment (through inability to learn from experience)

Thinking along these lines can assist the evaluator in making the connection between mental abnormality and volitional impairment. In either case, the evaluator must find signs that the mental abnormality impaired volition. For that, the various indicators reviewed in Chapter 2 are helpful.

Considering a Null Hypotheses

In line with our recommendation for hypothesis testing, the evaluator should consider what evidence would support a finding that no volitional impairment was present regarding the evaluee's sex offense(s). This is analogous to determining the signs one would need to see to accept the *null hypothesis* on the evaluee. Although one cannot prove a null hypothesis, one can at least articulate when the evidence is insufficient to establish that volitional impairment was present. This evidence may simply be a lack of the numerous possible indicators of volitional impairment.

Formulating an Opinion on Risk

The final component of SVP evaluations involves forming an opinion on increased risk. This determination may be specific to the jurisdiction in which the case is heard. Different jurisdictions use different definitions for the threshold of likelihood required to meet the SVP standard. Moreover, even the meaning of the same word ("likely," for instance) may be interpreted differently in the case law of two jurisdictions. It is helpful to consult with experienced SVP evaluators in one's jurisdiction to determine the formal and informal norms that operate in this regard. It is also helpful to consult with an attorney or the state agency.

Historical Risk Factors

The most heavily researched risk factors are historical, static ones, in part because these are the easiest to obtain from archival data. Conroy and Murrie (2007) review and categorize these risk factors as follows:

1. *Prior sexual offenses.* Given that, all else being equal, past behavior is the best predictor of future behavior, an individual with a long history of sex offenses would present higher risk than an individual with a shorter history of such offending. In addition, a past history of general violent, nonsexual offending has been found to be related to future sex offending.

2. *Deviant sexual interests.* This construct has been criticized as being imprecisely defined. In research studies, it usually refers to sexual interest in children or in torturing or humiliating one's victim.

3. *Psychopathy.* Typically assessed by scoring the PCL-R, this construct has two broad factors: callous, exploitive attitudes towards others and a chaotic, antisocial lifestyle. It overlaps with but is distinct from antisocial personality disorder.

4. *Antisocial lifestyle.* A generally antisocial lifestyle, including impulsivity, instability, and rule violations, has also been found to be associated with future sex offending.

6
chapter

5. *Age.* All else being equal, younger offenders, especially those between 18 and 30 years old, have higher recidivism rates than do older offenders. Above age 60, the sex offense recidivism rate drops dramatically.

6. *Sex and relationship.* Those offenders who molest unrelated and male victims have higher recidivism rates. Those who molest strangers also have higher recidivism rates.

7. *Past failures.* A history of failure to complete treatment or cooperate with legal supervision is associated with higher recidivism. (pp. 186–189)

In practice, however, in many jurisdictions, elevated risk involves consideration of an evaluee's scores on a standardized risk assessment instrument, along with an adjustment by the evaluator of risk or protective factors specific to that case. A recent factor analysis (Knight & Thornton, 2007) of a number of actuarial scales found five factors quite similar to those reviewed by Conroy and Murrie (2007). These factors were identified as criminal persistence, sexual persistence, being young and single, violent sexual assault, and male victim choice.

However, no risk assessment scale score can fully address the question of risk without other information. Although a risk assessment may have its foundation in a nomothetic scale, there is also the consideration of idiographic factors that are specific and perhaps unique to the case at hand. We do not recommend blind reliance on any nomothetic scale score. Even a rigorously developed actuarial scale, such as the Static-99, presumably measures underlying personal characteristics of the offender, and it is these characteristics, not just a scale score, that raise the likelihood for recidivism. A recent study (Craig, Thornton, Beech, & Browne, 2007) found that Static-99 items cluster into three broad areas—sexual deviance, general criminality, and immaturity—and it is these underlying personality attributes in which the evaluator is interested.

BEST PRACTICE

Do not rely simply on nomothetic scale scores, but assess the following underlying personality attributes:

● Sexual deviance

● General criminality

● Immaturity

In some jurisdictions, such as Texas, additional scales are considered that, although not formal risk assessment scales, have empirical relationships with recidivism. The Hare PCL-R is a good example of such a scale. Although it was not specifically developed to assess sex offense risk, it does positively correlate with recidivism (Barbaree, Seto, Langton, & Peacock, 2001; Hanson & Bussiere, 1998; Hanson & Morton-Bourgon, 2004; Harris, Rice, & Quinsey, 1998; Hildebrand, 2004; Langton, Barbaree, Harkins, & Peacock, 2006; Quinsey, Lalumiere, Rice, & Harris, 1995; Serin, Mailloux, & Malcolm, 2001; Seto & Barbaree, 1999).

> **BEWARE**
> Limitations of risk assessment scales include the following:
>
> - Historical risk factors are by nature static.
> - They provide an incomplete picture of risk.
> - The range of scores may be restricted.

Actuarial risk assessment scales, particularly the Static-99, focus heavily on historical risk factors. Such static, historical risk factors are well researched, and a good risk assessment should be anchored in them. However, complete reliance on historical risk factors results in important limitations. First, such factors, by definition, cannot change (or can change very little). Items such as number of victims or prior charges are unlikely to change during an evaluee's length of incarceration, except perhaps in the unusual case in which the evaluee actually commits a new sex offense while incarcerated. Moreover, such static, historical risk factors by necessity provide an incomplete picture of the evaluee's risk. Campbell (2004) has accurately noted that current actuarial risk assessment scales do not include static protective factors and dynamic risk or protective factors, although to include such factors it would need to be clearly demonstrated that they are empirically related to risk.

There is another difficulty in some jurisdictions: restricted range on actuarial risk assessment scales. In some states only a small minority of individuals initially screened for SVP commitment are actually committed. In such states, the select group referred for an actual SVP evaluation—that is, those who have gotten through the initial screening—all have elevated risk assessment screening scale scores. If there is a requirement (for example, due to space or funding restrictions) that only a given small proportion of evaluees be committed, then distinguishing that small percentage of evaluees appropriate for SVP commitment may need to be based on factors other than an elevated actuarial risk scale score, a characteristic that most evaluees will share.

Dynamic Risk Factors

Most commonly, additional information beyond that obtained from an actuarial risk assessment scale involves consideration of dynamic risk factors. Because static risk factors cannot change significantly, they are most useful for a one-time snapshot of the individual's risk, but less useful for evaluating change in risk over time or for developing a risk management plan. Here, dynamic (potentially changeable through planned intervention) risk factors are particularly important. Meta-analytic studies (Hanson & Harris, 1998, 2000; Hanson & Morton-Bourgon, 2004, 2005) suggest that the following dynamic risk factors may eventually prove to be useful in estimating the risk for sexual reoffending:

- Quality of social supports
- Emotional congruence or preoccupation with children
- Attitudes tolerant of sexual abuse
- Antisocial lifestyle
- Poor self-management
- Hostility
- Substance abuse
- Poor cooperation with supervision
- Employment instability
- General sexual preoccupation

Two instruments are useful in organizing dynamic risk factors. The first, the Sex Offender Need Assessment Rating (SONAR; Hanson & Harris, 1998, 2000), is organized very much along the above lines. A second instrument, the Structured Risk Assessment (SRA; Knight & Thornton, 2007) has a similar organization, consisting of sexual interests, distorted attitudes, socioaffective functioning, and self-management. Like other tools, these should serve as guides that are useful for helping the evaluator's thinking and organizing the findings clearly. However, relative to static risk factor research, the empirical study of dynamic risk factors is less extensive and more recent. The evaluator should be aware of the relative novelty of such dynamic risk assessment instruments and their research. Rather than relying extensively on such instruments for SVP evaluations, we can expect that with continued work in this area, dynamic risk assessment instruments may prove more helpful in the future—when their research base has expanded.

One potential advantage to using some form of structured professional judgment scale, such as the SVR-20, is that unlike strict actuarial scales, a research-based, structured, professional judgment instrument usually includes some dynamic risk factors. The SVR-20, for example, includes dynamic criteria that assess the quality of the individual's future plans and the presence (or absence) of a negative attitude towards intervention. In this way, a structured professional judgment instrument includes idiographic factors, as we will discuss later. Although structured professional judgment instruments cannot always be scored from archival records and typically require an interview, this is not necessarily a barrier in SVP cases, since an interview is generally conducted with (or at least offered to) the evaluee. A recent analysis by DeClue (2004) suggests that use of a structured professional judgment measure, such as the SVR-20, may well be admissible in *Frye* states even if used solely as an organizing structure. He notes,

> My review of the literature convinces me that the SVR-20 has emerged from the twilight zone: its potential to enhance the accuracy of sexually violent risk assessment is well established, it has gained general acceptance among well-trained forensic psychologists, and therefore the SVR-20 is now *Frye* admissible. (2004, p. 11)

Lack of Risk Factors

The evaluator should consider what risk factors the evaluee does not display. After all, the absence of risk factors is likely to lead to an opinion that the individual is not committable. Consider the following vignette, in which the lack of risk factors leads to an opinion that the individual does not meet the risk threshold for SVP commitment (despite the presence of an Axis I diagnosis, in this case, alcohol dependence and possibly sexual sadism as well, although the duration criterion for sexual sadism is not met).

> Mr. H. has engaged in one limited episode of sexual offending. His behavior during this offense illustrated deviant interests in which he used a weapon and deliberately inflicted pain, threatened to inflict pain, and intentionally humiliated his victim. Those who express deviant sexual interests have a higher probability of reoffending than that of other sex offenders; however, this offense does not appear to represent a pattern of behavior. His illegal actions were limited to one circumscribed episode.
>
> Mr. H's behavior during this offense was fueled by extensive alcohol abuse, and he has a history of alcohol dependence. Those who abuse substances, particularly at the time of relevant offenses, have a higher probability of reoffending than do other sexual offenders, should they continue to abuse substances. Mr. H. has not had an opportunity to violate probation, parole, or bond, but has left an alcohol treatment center against medical advice, raising concerns about his ability to refrain from alcohol use, particularly given the severity of his prior alcohol dependence.
>
> There are some risk factors for sexual reoffending that Mr. H. does not exhibit. There is no evidence of a history of criminal behavior other than the current offense. He has no male victims and no stranger victims. Being 52 years old, he is now past the age of greatest risk for reoffending, sexually or otherwise. In fact, rates of sexual offending recidivism are markedly lower for individuals his age and older. Although he has not been married, he has demonstrated the ability to establish an appropriate relationship with an adult female and has cohabited with a woman for 4 years. Mr. H. received a prorated score of 4.2 on the PCL-R, the most accurate current measure of psychopathy. Data indicate that a score above 30 is a strong predictor of violent recidivism; however, Mr. H. scores well below this range.
>
> Consequently, based on the information presented above, Mr. H. appears to be at low risk for reoffending, either generally or sexually. He appears to have a viable plan to stay away from alcohol;

however, his risk for recidivism in general is likely to increase if he continues to abuse alcohol in the future. For Mr. H., continued avoidance of alcohol use is important for him to avoid reoffending.

One can see the systematic consideration of risk factors in this example, both those factors present and those absent. Despite the reasoning that led to the conclusion that the evaluee did not meet the criteria for SVP commitment, however, his hypothetical Static-99 score would have been moderately elevated—a score of 4 in this example. This should underscore the policy consideration that when fine discriminations must be made within a group of individuals, all of whom have elevated actuarial scores, the risk scale can serve as a screening instrument only.

Idiographic Data

Although nomothetic evaluation forms a foundation for assessing risk, the evaluator should also tailor the risk assessment to account for idiographic data. As Conroy and Murrie note,

> to endorse idiographic assessment is not to endorse assessment by way of feelings, intuition, or vague clinical impressions. Rather, idiographic assessment involves carefully reviewing the offender's history, particularly as related to sexual offenses, and considering the future circumstances into which the person is likely to be placed. (2007, p. 192)

There may also be factors that have not been well researched but nevertheless apply to the specific individual being evaluated. For instance, although Axis I disorders other than paraphilias and substance abuse are infrequent in SVP cases, a particular case may involve an Axis I disorder. We evaluated one man with no prior history of criminal activity, sexual or otherwise, who masturbated in the presence of an underage male while in a manic state. Although diagnosis of bipolar mood disorder is not a generally supported risk factor, in this particular case, it was the primary risk factor. He showed no other inclination to commit illegal sexual behavior. When the offender's mood disorder was properly treated, his risk was minimal, as demonstrated by decades of offense-free community adjustment since the time of his offense. Conroy and Murrie (2007) also noted a case in

6
chapter

BEST PRACTICE
To develop a risk man-
agement plan, conduct an
idiographic functional analysis.

which a man had committed a sex offense while in an acute psychotic state, but not otherwise. Hence, although psychosis is not a generally supported risk factor in the literature, it did serve as a risk factor for that particular offender.

In addition, sex offenses occur in a specific context. Even an individual who scores high on a static risk assessment scale will commit sex offenses in some situational contexts and not in others. In a cogent discussion of this point, Beech and Ward (2004) proposed that traits (or stable dynamic risk factors) lead to historical markers (static risk factors). These traits are triggered in specific situational contexts, resulting in negative affect and, in the end, the commission of a sex offense. Beech, Fisher, and Thornton (2003) recommended a detailed functional analysis of the motives, thoughts, situational precipitants, and reward and punishment contingencies associated with the offender's history of sex offending. Such an idiographic functional analysis can add greatly to the usefulness of a risk assessment. At some time, presumably, many of the individuals committed under SVP statutes will eventually be released into the community. Moreover, many individuals evaluated for SVP commitment will not, in fact, be committed. In some jurisdictions, all that is needed and required is an opinion on whether the individual is committable. In other jurisdictions, the court expects that a risk management plan be developed for those individuals. In such cases, a detailed functional analysis, including a discussion of the contexts in which offenses are likely to occur, will help in developing such a plan.

Summary

In this chapter, we first address the issues involved in formulating opinions generally. The evaluator must carefully consider what factual foundation she is using and what conceptually connects those facts to the inferences the evaluator is drawing. We recommend that the evaluator be quite explicit in articulating both the underlying facts and the possible hypotheses that may account for these facts. The evaluator can then systematically describe the consistency between the facts and different hypotheses. We recommend a slight modification of the three-stage sequence proposed by Heilbrun and colleagues (2002).

- First, identify the relevant legal construct.

- Second, determine how these constructs can be measured and what methods might be used to measure them.

- Third, gather information in the relevant domains to assess these constructs.

- Fourth, use the information gathered to form and test hypotheses concerning the fit of the facts to the legal constructs.

Finally, we discuss the considerations involved in formulating opinions on each aspect of the three psycholegal constructs involved in SVP evaluations—mental disorder, volitional impairment, and risk.

Report Writing and Testimony | 7

An evaluation conducted for the purpose of assisting the trier of fact in determining whether someone should be committed as a sexually violent predator is, by its nature, a forensic mental health assessment. It should include all of the elements required in such an endeavor and abide by the appropriate practice guidelines (see Heilbrun, Grisso, & Goldstein, 2008, the first book in this series).

Introductory Elements

Reason for Referral

FMHA reports often begin with a statement of the reason for referral (Groth-Marnat, 2003). This would be a statement of the purpose of the evaluation and the question or questions the evaluator intends to address. It may also specify an evaluator's intent to assist the court in determining whether the individual should be committed as a sexually violent predator rather than to reach a particular ultimate issue conclusion. The agency or individual for whom the work was conducted should also be specified.

Consent or Disclosure

Reports should document the consent or disclosure provided to the evaluee and the elements included (e.g., purpose of the evaluation, limits of confidentiality, access to the results). Some evaluators routinely attach a copy of the written consent or disclosure to the final report. It is often helpful to include information relevant to the individual's response. Did the person display a clear understanding of the information? Were pertinent questions asked? Was the individual willing to participate? If the individual refused to participate, was a reason given?

Collateral Information

Each source of collateral information directly pertaining to the case at hand should be listed. Evaluators should be explicit in listing documents and describe them in sufficient detail so they can be easily identified by the reader (e.g., title, source, date). It is also helpful during testimony if documents are listed in an easily retrievable order. Ordinarily, this will not include reference materials such as published research; if a specific publication is cited in the report, it can be referenced in a list at the end of the report. Attorneys sometimes request a detailed list of any material relied upon prior to a legal proceeding, and this can be provided separately. In addition to documents, any video or audiotapes reviewed should be cited. If the evaluator has interviewed third parties, all names, the dates of interviews, and medium (i.e., telephone, in person) should be provided. If collateral information of any kind is provided to the evaluator and reviewed, it should be included on the list—even if it is minimally relevant to the final report.

Procedures

All procedures undertaken as part of the assessment should be listed. This would include documenting the date, location, and duration of all interviews or attempted interviews. If psychological tests, risk assessment tools, or structured interviews were employed, these should be listed. Finally, it is important to note if any recording devices, either audio or video, were used during the evaluation. If the evaluation is recorded, in part or in its entirety, this recording should be maintained as part of the record.

Background Information

Jurisdiction Requirements

Jurisdictions vary widely on what is expected in evaluation reports for SVP proceedings. It is not unusual for reports in states such as Minnesota and California to reach 40 or 50 single-spaced pages, because evaluators typically provide background information by first summarizing each document that was reviewed. In jurisdictions such as Texas, however, reports are more likely to be five to six pages. Given that all referenced documents are fully discoverable, writers in Texas simply incorporate relevant information into the main report. It is probably wise for new evaluators to investigate the expected format in the particular jurisdiction.

Length of Report

Although evaluators should be aware of the expectations in their jurisdictions, we recommend that the information included in such evaluations and the ultimate length of reports be guided by relevance to the constructs being assessed. For documents in the file with little or no relevance for the evaluation, we suggest that summarizing and including such documents is not a good use of the evaluator's time, nor of the court's or attorneys' time. We have observed that reports of extreme length, with a good deal of marginally relevant to irrelevant material, tempt the reader to review only the conclusions section. (For jurisdictions in which there is a clear expectation that "all" the information be included, we suggest that the evaluator use a lengthy appendix containing the information that is expected but not relevant to the report proper.)

Confidentiality and Red-Herring Data

From a best-practice perspective, reports would include a thorough discussion of relevant background information. Grisso (1998) advised all forensic evaluators to "include all data that are necessary in order to support or question your opinion (p. 249)." Any information relating to a known risk or protective factor would be relevant. Beyond that, however, the *Specialty Guidelines for Forensic Psychologists* emphasize the importance of making "every effort to maintain confidentiality with regard to any information that does not bear directly upon the legal purpose of the evaluation" (Committee on Ethical Guidelines for Forensic Psychologists, 1991, p. 660). In this regard, Conroy and Murrie (2007) caution evaluators against including "red herring" data that "have no demonstrable bearing on risk level and that distract from a risk opinion rooted in nomothetic data and relevant idiographic data" (p. 121). Examples might include salacious or sensational-sounding information about the evaluee's family members or the victim. In the course of

BEWARE
Be cautious when including red-herring data in the report that may lead the reader to overestimate risk.

taking a sexual history, the evaluator will address the evaluee's history of healthy sexual relationships, and knowledge of these relationships is helpful in providing a broad perspective on the evaluee's overall sexual interest and behavior pattern. However, the evaluator should be cautious about focusing on and reporting salacious or sensationalistic material, if such material is not clearly germane to the evaluation.

Another type of red-herring data would involve lengthy discussions of factors that may be mistakenly viewed as risk factors. For example, it may be inappropriate to include lengthy discussions of an evaluee's adamant denial of past offenses. This might leave the impression that this variable is predictive of future risk when research has found no such correlation (Hanson & Bussiere, 1998). However, it might also be important to briefly acknowledge the denial lest the audience think the evaluator is unaware of it. A useful guideline in determining the details of an individual's background that should be included is to consider how much the detail informs the evaluator's opinion.

Language

The impact of any background information can be altered by the language in which it is couched. Evaluators should keep in mind the obligation to provide information in as fair and objective a manner as possible, "examining the issue at hand from all reasonable perspectives, actively seeking information that will differentially test plausible rival hypotheses" (Committee on Ethical Guidelines for Forensic Psychologists, 1991, p. 661). Biased or inflammatory language is always to be avoided.

Mental Condition

In keeping with the U.S. Supreme Court's decision in *Kansas v. Hendricks* (1997), all SVP statutes mandate that the risk presented by a sexual offender subject to civil commitment must be rooted in some "condition," variously called "mental disorder," "mental abnormality," "personality

BEWARE
Be sure to avoid biased or inflammatory language.

disorder," "diagnosed mental illness," or "behavioral abnormality." This is one of the essential elements to be addressed by an evaluator. However, courts have consistently ruled that states have the right to define this condition as lawmakers choose and a diagnosis specifically described in the *Diagnostic and Statistical Manual, Fourth Edition, Text Revision* (*DSM-IV-TR*; American Psychiatric Association, 2000) is not required. Most jurisdictions have crafted legal language such as the following: "a congenital or acquired condition affecting the emotional or volitional capacity which predisposes the person to commit sexually violent offenses in a degree constituting such a person a menace to the health and safety of others" (Commitment of Sexually Violent Predators Act, 2002). Such legal language has no particular relationship to psychodiagnostic procedures used by mental health professionals. Nonetheless, it is generally recommended that forensic mental health professionals provide clinical diagnoses in the standard fashion, using the *DSM-IV-TR* (Association for the Treatment of Sexual Abusers, 1997; Miller, Amenta, & Conroy, 2005). To invent syndromes or clusters of symptoms in an attempt to conform to the legal definition would be to ignore any requirements for validity and reliability. Rather, it is essential that the evaluator begin by describing any bona fide clinical conditions that the individual may have and later make the necessary psycholegal connections.

Paraphilia

The most common diagnostic category used as the basis for an SVP commitment is paraphilia (Becker, Stinson, Tromp, & Messer, 2003). Some experts have argued that, given the nature of this commitment, some paraphilic diagnosis is essential (Becker & Murphy, 1998). However, in applying one of these diagnoses, evaluators must be very clear about what it actually means. The research base for these diagnoses is very weak (Miller et al., 2005). Most sexual disorders were ignored in field trials prior to the fourth edition of the *DSM* (O'Donohue, Regev, & Hagstrom, 2000). In addition, it can be seriously questioned whether a diagnosis such as pedophilia is any more than a description of behavior without benefit of pathology or etiology. Some legal experts have chastised the mental health community, suggesting that anyone who has an adequate record, can read the English language, and can count could arrive at this diagnosis (Schopp, Scalora, & Pearce, 1999). A person who is at least 16 years of age and has molested a child or children over at least a 6-month period has met the criteria for the diagnosis. Authors of the *DSM* included cautionary language, noting, "It is to be understood that inclusion here, for clinical and research purposes, of a diagnostic category such as Pathological Gambling or Pedophilia does not imply that the condition meets legal or other non-medical criteria for what constitutes mental disease, mental disorder, or mental disability" (p. xxxvii). Paraphilia NOS, a diagnosis sometimes applied by evaluators to anyone who has committed rape, is even more vaguely defined. Do the paraphilias ever go into remission as other mental disorders often do? This question becomes particularly salient when an individual has not evidenced the aberrant behavior for years, or even decades, but has been incarcerated during that time.

Personality Disorder

Personality disorder is the second most common diagnostic category to be relied upon during SVP evaluations. More research data and assessment tools (e.g., tests, structured instruments) have been developed in regard to personality disorders than relating to paraphilias. However, evaluators need to take great care in relating a particular personality disorder to a predisposition to commit sexual offenses. Antisocial personality disorder is the most frequent of the category to appear in SVP proceedings. Yet research would indicate that 40%–80% of incarcerated males qualify for this diagnosis (Cunningham & Reidy, 1998; Hare, 1998; Moran, 1999). The vast majority of these individuals are not convicted of a sexual offense.

Psychopathy

Psychopathy is not currently a *DSM* diagnosis. However, it has a strong research base indicating that it is predictive of both nonsexual violent and sexual reoffending (Barbaree, Seto, Langton, & Peacock, 2001; Hanson & Bussiere, 1998; Hanson & Morton-Bourgon,

2004; Langton, Barbaree, Harkins, & Peacock, 2006; Serin, Mailloux, & Malcolm, 2001). At least one state (Texas) requires assessment of psychopathy as part of all SVP evaluations. Regardless of its *DSM* status, the research base, in addition to the availability of a well-validated assessment tool, would make it relevant to any discussion of mental condition in this context.

Using DSM Diagnoses

One of the difficulties in determining appropriate diagnoses for an SVP report is deciding how to use *DSM* diagnoses. If one renders a diagnosis, it must be done in a way that is consistent with the recognized standards in the field. Also, any deviation from *DSM* diagnostic criteria can open the practitioner to intense cross-examination from the opposing attorney. However, the *DSM* was never written to be statutorily binding, but rather to be used a guide for clinical judgment. An important caveat in the preface should be familiar to anyone proffering diagnoses in a courtroom. The specific diagnostic criteria included in the *DSM-IV-TR* are meant

> to serve as guidelines to be informed by clinical judgment and not meant to be used in cookbook fashion. For example, the exercise of clinical judgment may justify giving a certain diagnosis to an individual even if the clinical presentation falls short of meeting the full criteria for the diagnosis as long as the symptoms that are present are persistent and severe. On the other hand, lack of familiarity with DSM-IV or excessive flexibility and idiosyncratic application of DSM-IV criteria or conventions substantially reduces its utility as a common language for communication. (APA, 2000, p. xxxii)

Even language commonly used by experts in reports (i.e., symptoms meet the criteria for . . .) may further imply to the court that these criteria are inflexible and either met (in which case the diagnosis must be applied) or not met (in which case the diagnosis cannot be given). In reality, evaluators must use clinical judgment in reaching the most appropriate diagnoses. For example, for an individual convicted of molesting a 13-year-old female in January and again 7 months later, it is important to note that the offenses occurred some time ago, the person has been living in the community since

7
chapter

BEST PRACTICE
Use clinical judgment in making a diagnosis and be prepared to defend any deviation from *DSM* criteria.

then, and appears to have led an otherwise normal sexual life. Depending on other information, the evaluator may determine that this example would not constitute a chronic pattern of behavior and does not warrant a diagnosis of pedophilia. By contrast, consider an individual found to have molested dozens of prepubescent boys during 3 months serving as a counselor at a summer camp, but has no other established history of sexual offending. The evaluator may conclude in this case that the frequency and intensity of the individual's sexual behavior with minors qualify him for a finding of pedophilia, despite the short duration, a conclusion not totally in keeping with *DSM* criteria. It is critical that the evaluator think through any diagnosis carefully and be prepared to defend it in light of the *DSM*, particularly if the evaluator concludes that there are good reasons for deviating from the explicit *DSM* criteria in the case.

As with any other forensic evaluation, mental health professionals assessing someone as part of SVP proceedings should include a careful explanation connecting the specific person to any diagnosis given. Contrary evidence also must be openly addressed. Finally, if there is reason to believe the person is suspected of having a disorder but the evaluator concluded that this disorder is not present, the evaluator may need to explain why the evaluator concluded that there were not sufficient data to show that the person meets criteria for the diagnosis.

Risk Assessment

Over the past 20 years, there has been a great deal of research in the area of risk assessment. Indeed, there has been so much research that it is challenging for the clinician practicing in this arena to identify work that is most relevant and remain current on emerging research.

Base Rates

Many risk assessment reports include a discussion of base rates among the relevant population. Monahan (1981) stressed that base rates may be the most important element in the prediction of

BEWARE
There are inherent difficulties in calculating accurate base rates in sex offense cases. If citing base rates, include a cautionary note to this effect.

violence and ignoring base rates may be the most egregious error that clinicians make. However, this may not be a feasible strategy in evaluating risk among sexual offenders. Attempts to calculate accurate base rates for reoffense have been compromised by an inconsistent application of criteria, the plethora of unreported offenses, the extended period over which some offenders reoffend, and the tendency of some evaluators to assume that sexual offenders constitute a homogeneous population. If base rates are cited in a report, as they might well be if using an instrument for which such base rates have been compiled (such as the Static-99), it would be wise to include a cautionary note regarding the difficulties inherent in calculating accurate base rates in sex offense cases. (For a more complete discussion, see Chapter 3.)

Risk Factors

In most cases, an SVP report will need to include discussion of the most well-established risk factors for sexual reoffending. A number of factors have been well researched and repeatedly found to be predictive, both in individual studies and in meta-analyses. (For a more thorough review see Chapter 3 of this volume; see also Conroy & Murrie, 2007). Most of the strongly supported factors currently researched are static in nature. However, that may be quite appropriate for initial SVP evaluations, as risk management plans are rarely required. In cases of evaluations that consider potential discharge from confinement and recommend potential conditions of release, both static and dynamic risk factors should be addressed.

Idiographic Analysis

The population of sexual offenders is a very heterogeneous group. It should not be assumed that all empirically supported risk factors operate in the same way with every person or that all of the important risk factors for everyone have been identified. Rather, it would be good practice to include relevant idiographic analysis in SVP reports. This is not to say that the evaluator relies on unconfirmed clinical intuition, feelings, or hunches. An idiographic analysis

7
chapter

means examining the individual's past offenses in detail to ascertain what might have contributed to or precipitated the behavior and under what circumstances (Beech, Fisher, & Thornton, 2003; Conroy & Murrie, 2007). Established risk and protective factors do not necessarily operate the same way in every person. Consider, for example, the person who commits his first sexual offense at age 45 and the behavior continues to escalate until he is finally incarcerated at age 59. In this case, advancing age does not seem to result in lower risk. Maintaining a satisfactory long-term relationship with an appropriate adult partner has generally been found to be inversely related to risk for recidivism. However, this may not apply if the spouse is a willing accomplice in perpetrating the sexual offenses. In rare instances, an Axis I diagnosis may be the most prominent risk factor for a particular person. Consider, for example, someone who perpetrates sexual offenses in response to delusional beliefs. Treatment recommendations could be critical in this instance, but would likely not emphasize any of the traditional sex offender programs. A final type of case requiring this kind of analysis is that in which something critical has changed in the individual or circumstances—Meehl's "broken leg" phenomenon (see, e.g., Grove & Meehl, 1996). For example, would it make a difference if the offender was injured and rendered quadriplegic? Would it matter if the individual lost his sight? What about the person who has just been sentenced to 20 years in prison?

Risk Assessment Instruments

Evaluators will often use instruments especially designed to assess risk in this population (see Chapter 3 for a review of such instruments). Courts and attorneys, with the exception of those who specialize in this area of law, will generally be unfamiliar with these measures. Any instrument used should be briefly described in the report with respect to its nature and purpose; a more elaborate description is unnecessary. Rather, the evaluator should be familiar with the psychometric properties of any instrument employed and prepared to explain them in layman's language if asked.

Communicating to the Court About Risk

Prior to 1990, there was virtually no research on how best to communicate information about risk to the trier of fact. However, as emphasized by Heilbrun, Dvoskin, Hart, and McNeil (1999), risk communication is a critical variable:

> Assessments of risk are valuable to the extent that they can improve legal or clinical decisions. . . . The only way risk assessors can influence decisions is by effectively communicating the findings to the legal and clinical actors whose decisions they wish to influence. (p. 94)

Methods of Communicating Risk

Methods of communicating level of risk have generally been categorized into three different formats. The first of these is *categorical*. This is the most common way of expressing risk as simply *low, moderate,* or *high* (Heilbrun, Philipson, Berman, & Warren, 1999). Some have added additional categories or subdivided categories. Monahan and Steadman (1996) proposed an analogy in which risk communication would be categorical, with implications for action linked with each category, as is done in forecasting severe weather events. They suggested "no warning" (no implications for action), "watch" (observe and prepare), and "warning" (take immediate action) in analogizing weather communication to level of violence risk.

In the second method numerical probability is used to estimate the risk that a violent event will occur. For example, one might say, "This offender has a 45% probability of reoffending." The Violence Risk Appraisal Guide (VRAG) offers actuarial results in this format, estimating the probability that an individual scoring in a certain range will be violent over a specific period of time (Quinsey et al., 1998, 2006). Monahan and Steadman (1996) predicted that this would be used to a greater extent as measurement becomes more precise.

Finally, risk can be communicated using numerical frequency. For example, one might say, "Research suggests that out of 100 men

7
chapter

similar to this offender, 20 are likely to commit a violent act." The numerical methods may seem initially attractive, as research has shown considerable variability in the way people interpret low, moderate, or high risk (Kwartner, Lyons, & Boccaccini, 2006). Numerical expression would seem to be more standard, as it might seem obvious that 20% means exactly the same thing as 20 out of 100. However, researchers have found that when the two were compared, a frequency estimate seemed to indicate higher risk than the same estimate expressed as a percentage, perhaps because those hearing risk communicated in categories are more apt to imagine those 20 cases in the numerator (Monahan et al., 2002; Slovic, Monahan, & MacGregor, 2000).

Method Preferences

CLINICIANS

When clinicians were asked which approach they preferred, most indicated that they avoided numerical estimates, saying they could not possibly be that precise with data currently available (Heilbrun, Philipson, et al., 1999; Heilbrun, O'Neill, Strohman, Bowman, & Philipson, 2000; Heilbrun et al., 2004). This response is consistent with views expressed by Monahan and Steadman (1996), who observed, "clinicians may find it both pretentious and potentially misleading to produce risk assessments along a 100-point probability scale" (p. 935).

Clinicians seemed most supportive of presenting risk assessment results in the context of risk management, endorsing statements such as, "Mr. Smith's risk of committing an act of violence toward others will depend upon (risk factor) and whether (intervention) can be put in place to address the problem." Heilbrun et al. (2000) observed that clinicians may be more supportive of a prediction model in high-risk situations where risk factors tend to be static, but turn to a model based on management when risk factors are more dynamic.

COURTS

Although it is interesting to know the preferences of clinicians, the courts are the primary consumer of risk assessment communications. Many observers have agreed that courts have historically tended to be very skeptical of statistics and social science data in general (Bersoff & Glass, 1995; Melton et al., 2007; Redding, 1998; Slobogin, 1998; Tanford, 1990). Following a review of federal judicial opinions, Fradella, Fogarty, and O'Neill (2003) concluded that courts' resistance to social science was an increasing trend throughout the 1990s. To date, Kwartner and colleagues (2006) have published the only data directly relating to judge's preferences for risk communication formats. In a survey of 116 judges, they found the majority preferred categorical reporting.

JURORS

It would seem that if judges are skeptical of statistical data then jurors, who are generally less educated and sophisticated as a group than judges, would be even more so. As with much of the research regarding juries, it should be kept in mind that research done in this arena used college students as mock jurors and may not translate fully to the behavior of actual jurors. Some research would suggest that mock jurors were more persuaded by unstructured clinical judgment than by actuarial assessment (Krauss & Sales, 2001; Krauss & Lee, 2003). This would seem to call into question the assertion by Justice White in the case of *Barefoot v. Estelle* (1983) regarding the ability of the adversary system to unmask any flaws in mental health testimony:

> We are not persuaded that such testimony is almost entirely unreliable and that the factfinder and the adversary system will not be competent to uncover, recognize, and take due account of its shortcomings. (p. 899)

Role of Educator

The previous discussion is not to suggest that evaluators present reports in terms of clinical pronouncements to the exclusion of scientific data. Rather, it indicates that evaluators must, to some degree, assume the role of educators. Respectfully and without being condescending or overly technical, reports should communicate not only the relevant data but also the rationale behind the procedures used.

Jurors or judges, when confronted with research data (which may appear unrelated to the particular offender), may ask, "Why should I care?" The evaluator must be prepared to answer that question.

The degree to which an evaluator needs to provide education, of course, will depend on the sophistication of the audience. For example, in some jurisdictions, large numbers of SVP cases are heard by the same courts, and judges may become very knowledgeable about the science in the area. Although critically important, research data should not be the total focus of a report. It is also essential that case-specific, idiographic data be included to bring the findings together and relate them directly to the individual.

Communicating Types of Risk

Reports should also make very clear the type of risk that is assessed. For example, the same individual may be at a different level of risk for sexual reoffending than for nonsexual violent offending. In some cases it may not be possible to distinguish the type of offense most probable with any reasonable degree of clinical certainty. Statements may need to use language such as the following: "For all of the reasons detailed here, in my opinion Mr. Jones is at very high risk for committing violence in the future; however, there is no way to determine the likelihood that his reoffending would be sexual in nature."

In considering types of risk, evaluators must also be aware of the jurisdiction's definitions of "predatory." In some states (e.g., Missouri, Washington), predatory behavior is defined as acts in which the victim is a stranger, a very casual acquaintance, or someone with whom a relationship was established for the specific purpose of victimization. For example, Washington's SVP statute (RCW 71.09.020) states: "Predatory means acts directed towards: (a) strangers; (b) individuals with whom a relationship has been established or promoted for the primary purpose of victimization; or (c) persons of casual

BEWARE
Be cautious
of planning
interventions that are not
empirically established to
reduce recidivism.

acquaintance with whom no substantial personal relationship exists." This definition would eliminate a large number of intrafamilial offenses.

Communicating About Risk Management

In cases where a release to the community under some specified conditions is an option, inclusion of risk management recommendations may be appropriate. Three commonly applied models of risk management for sexual offenders have been identified: (a) a sex offender treatment program, (b) a medication regimen, and (c) a containment approach (applying every conceivable intervention to every offender). However, when these approaches are applied indiscriminantly, they fail to recognize the heterogeneity of the sex offender population and, consequently, may not adequately address the needs of the individual (Conroy, 2006).

A small body of literature on violence risk management has begun to emerge regarding methods of formulating a risk management plan (Andrews & Bonta, 2003; Conroy, 2006; Conroy & Murrie, 2007; Heilbrun, 1997). The first step is to identify the major factors, both nomothetic and idiographic, that put the individual at risk for future violence. Next, the evaluator must determine which factors are amenable to intervention and then determine strategies that have been proven to be effective.

Risk management plans will only be effective if they are grounded in science. Perhaps the most prominent error in risk management planning is the development of interventions around common wisdom or illusory correlations that are not supported by available data. For example, in the case of sex offenders, plans often emphasize the breakdown of denial or building victim empathy. In reality, these elements have not been empirically established as related to recidivism risk (Hanson & Bussiere, 1998; Hanson & Morton-Bourgon, 2004). A second problem may arise if evaluators rely too heavily on their own professional discipline. For example, counseling or psychotherapy may not be the most appropriate intervention to mitigate a risk factor and is certainly not the only solution. Effective risk management plans will generally involve interdisciplinary collaboration (Douglas, Webster, Hart, Eaves, & Ogloff, 2001). Finally,

7
chapter

BEWARE
Do not score
an instrument
without sufficient
information.

if an evaluator is recommending an untried intervention or one for which the outcome data have been variable, this should be clearly stated. In such cases, it would be important to explain why the strategy is apt to reduce risk for the particular target individual.

Limitations

Every evaluation has limitations, and significant limitations should be specified in reports. One of the most common problems encountered is a dearth of reliable records. Either certain key records cannot be obtained at all, or it is not possible to verify important information, or the inconsistencies cannot be reasonably explained. Each evaluator must determine whether opinions can be rendered at all with available information and what caveats need to be attached. If using instruments such as the PCL-R, sufficient collateral information should be available or no score should be calculated. It is better to explain to the court that an instrument could not be reliably scored than to attempt scoring with insufficient information. An instrument should not be used if sufficient information is not available.

Another common limitation is lack of access to or full participation from the subject of the evaluation. Any such limitations, and attempts to address them, should be documented. Any cultural factors that limit communication should also be noted, as well as any use of interpreters.

Finally, if risk management is included, it should always be recognized that some risk factors—particularly those that are static in nature—cannot be remediated. For example, nothing can reduce the person's history of offending or history of violating past conditions of release. Someone found to be high in psychopathic traits is unlikely to experience radical personality change. Risk management, by definition, indicates that risk cannot be eliminated. How much risk is tolerable is an issue for the trier of fact to determine.

The Ultimate Issue

The issue of whether mental health professionals should address the ultimate legal issue at all in a forensic report has been highly controversial (Melton et al., 2007). However, this issue takes on special significance in SVP proceedings because of the largely nonclinical nature of the standards as written.

The first element is the condition or disorder. As defined in statutes, this would appear to have no direct relationship to any clinical diagnosis contained in the *DSM-IV-TR* or otherwise supported by a research base (e.g., psychopathy). Reviewing the clinical criteria for diagnoses most commonly used in SVP proceedings—paraphilias and personality disorders—it would appear difficult to establish the etiology or pathology underlying the condition.

INFO

If addressing the ultimate issue, three elements to consider are the following:

● Presence of a mental condition or disorder

● Whether the condition results in some particular difficulty controlling the target behavior

● Risk assessment and, in some jurisdictions, risk management

The second element is that the condition results in some particular difficulty in controlling the target behavior. U.S. Supreme Court rulings in *Kansas v. Hendricks* (1997) and *Kansas v. Crane* (2002), as well as state case law that followed (e.g., *In re Leon G.* [2002]; *In re Martinelli,* [2002]; *In re Thorell* [2003]) made clear that the condition or disorder needed to be related to the behavioral control problem in order to distinguish the person subject to commitment from other offenders. As documented in Chapter 3, the clinical sciences have not found valid methods of distinguishing volitional impairment from a choice to engage in aberrant behavior. Arguments can be made from logic and common sense that if someone fails to control behavior, even in the face of repeated negative consequences, then perhaps he has special difficulty with control. However, the expert is not summoned to explain common sense but rather to assist the trier of fact with information that is beyond the understanding of the layperson.

The final element is risk. The mental health profession has a large volume of data that may be very helpful to the trier of fact in this area. Clinicians' interviewing skills and training in analyzing a person's behavioral history can also add value. In many cases risk assessment, as well as risk management planning, can be based in solid science and professional expertise. However, clinicians should

7
chapter

think carefully before proffering an ultimate issue opinion asserting certainty on all three elements and their interrelationship.

Presenting Courtroom Testimony

Much has been written for mental health professionals by experienced forensic examiners about how best to prepare for and engage in court-room testimony (Bank & Packer, 2007; Barsky & Gould, 2002; Brodsky, 1991, 1999; Hess, 2006; Lubet, 1998; Ziskin & Faust, 1995). Although oral and written communications differ in style, much of what has been said about constructing reports and the content thereof would also apply to courtroom testimony. Three additional topics in regard to the courtroom will be addressed here: qualifications, evidentiary standards, and preparation with an attorney.

Qualifications

The court determines who is allowed to testify as an expert, generally on the basis of "knowledge, skill, experience, training, or education" (Federal Rule of Evidence 702). Unless the witness is well known to the court and all parties stipulate to her qualifications, testimony is often prefaced by an examination of the witness as to her credentials and qualifications. However, the mental health professional retains a responsibility for seeing that qualifications are fairly and honestly presented to the court.

> III. B. Forensic psychologists have an obligation to present to the court, regarding the specific matters to which they will testify, the boundaries of their competence, the factual bases (knowledge, skill, experience, training, and education) for their qualification as an expert, and the relevance of those factual bases to their qualification as an expert on the specific matters at issue. (Committee for Ethical Guidelines for Forensic Psychologists, 1991, p. 658)

Similar guidelines regarding accurate presentation of credentials to the courts exist for forensic psychiatrists:

> When providing expert opinion, reports, and testimony, psychiatrists should present their qualifications accurately and precisely. As a correlate of the principle that expertise may be appropriately claimed only

in areas of actual knowledge, skill, training and experience, there are areas of special expertise, such as the evaluation of children, persons of foreign cultures, or prisoners, that may require special training or expertise. (American Academy of Psychiatry and Law, 2005, p. 4)

Credentials generally include educational degrees, training, licensure, and board certification. Qualifications for testimony in a specific case, however, go well beyond credentials. The fact that an individual holds a doctoral degree and is licensed to practice psychology in a given jurisdiction does not necessarily mean that he is qualified to testify regarding the risk posed by a certain sex offender. Other issues commonly considered include experience working with sexual offenders, experience working with criminal and psychopathic populations, expertise in the science of risk assessment, training and experience using relevant instruments, and expertise in diagnosing relevant conditions.

> **INFO**
>
> Qualifications to consider for testimony as an expert include the following:
>
> - Credentials (e.g., degrees, licensure)
> - Work experience
> - Expertise in risk assessment
> - Familiarity with relevant instruments
> - Expertise in diagnosis
> - Experience relevant to the particular case

Before undertaking a case that could result in expert testimony, forensic clinicians should carefully consider their particular experience that would especially qualify them in a particular case. For example, working with a particular cultural population or speaking a language fluently may be relevant. It may also be appropriate to consider areas in which expertise is lacking and may be questioned. For example, it is not uncommon to be asked, "Do you regularly provide treatment to sexual offenders?" It is certainly not necessary to be a treatment provider to assess risk, but one may want to be prepared for the question.

Evidentiary Standards

Jurisdictions vary as to the standard by which courts admit expert evidence. This may be statutory (e.g., the Federal Rules of Evidence), but more often has been established in case law. It is important for witnesses to be aware of the standard to which their work may be held. The majority of jurisdictions rely on some variation of the *Frye* rule or

7
chapter

CASE LAW

Frye v. United States (1923)

- The DC Circuit Court of Appeals ruled that in order to be admitted into evidence, methodology needed to have "gained general acceptance in the particular field in which it belongs" (p. 1014).

- This case has guided legal thinking throughout the country for nearly 60 years and is still the rule in a number of jurisdictions.

Daubert v. Merrell Dow Pharmaceuticals, Inc. (1993)

- The U.S. Supreme Court suggested four criteria that a judge may want to consider in determining whether scientific evidence should be admitted:

  a. Has it been tested or is it testable?

  b. Has it been published or subject to peer review?

  c. Is there an established error rate?

  d. Is it generally accepted in the relevant field?

- Although the *Daubert* ruling itself only applied in federal courts, numerous jurisdictions have since adopted the approach.

- In some cases, a *Daubert* hearing may be conducted before the judge to determine the admissibility of particular evidence.

the *Daubert* criteria. These are most likely to become relevant when the witness has used a particular test or structured method.

In addition to the general evidentiary standards, SVP proceedings often present more specific concerns. For example, in Texas a *Daubert* hearing that stretched over several days was held in regard to the admissibility of actuarial risk assessment instruments. The result was a court ruling that sufficient scientific evidence supported the development of such devices that the jury could hear the evidence and make their own decision on the merits. Of course, this issue could be raised again in regard to newer devices.

Jurisdictions may also have rules regarding the admissibility of evidence obtained from testing with polygraphs or plethysmographs. Finally, in some jurisdictions testimony of a medical doctor (usually a psychiatrist) is required for commitment. This does not mean that other experts cannot testify, but they may not be able to offer an opinion specific to commitment. Overall, a thorough knowledge of the legal rules governing testimony is essential to effective expert testimony.

Preparation With an Attorney

Unlike the written report, courtroom testimony is almost always presented in a question-and-answer format. This means that the witness is dependent upon the examining attorney to pose questions that allow a thorough and organized presentation of the information and opinions that will be most helpful to the trier of fact. Under these circumstances, it is important that both the witness and the attorney share an understanding of the evidence the witness will offer and how it may best be explained. The most effective approach to facilitating this process is through solid preparation with the attorney who will be calling the witness. Direct examination is an opportunity to present one's findings to the court and provide explanation as needed. A well-prepared direct examination is also the best defense when it is time for cross-examination.

In addition to discussing the content to be presented, a preparation meeting gives the witness an opportunity to ask other questions. For example, the attorney may have knowledge of the judge and jury and the level of sophistication to be expected. Explaining complex material to the attorney (a layperson) may help the evaluator to become more aware of areas that will be difficult to explain in the courtroom. Attorneys can be helpful reframing difficult issues or in suggesting analogies, and often provide useful information on the type of cross-examination the witness should expect. Finally, it is important that the witness discuss with the attorney how the ultimate issue will—or will not—be addressed.

A great deal of work will have taken place prior to a courtroom appearance. However, the impact will be lost without a strong written report and effective presentation in the courtroom.

BEST PRACTICE

Have a preparation meeting with the attorney to

- Review the evidence to be examined in court
- Ask questions that may provide useful information
- Discuss how the ultimate issue will—or will not—be addressed

7
chapter

Conclusion

Communication of one's findings to the court through either a report or testimony draws on all the elements we have previously covered. In this final stage, the forensic evaluator ties together her review of typically voluminous records, tests, risk assessment findings, and interviews. From this information, she distills an opinion that addresses the psycholegal constructs of mental disorder, volitional impairment, and risk. In doing so, the evaluator bears in mind the extent to which empirical findings can guide opinions on each of these constructs. To avoid an overly lengthy report—one that lends itself to having only the conclusion read—the forensic evaluator needs to separate the relevant from the irrelevant in the report, focusing on those aspects of the case relevant to the psycholegal constructs under consideration. The forensic evaluator must have a command of diagnosis and clear knowledge of risk assessment methods, including the limits of each. Perhaps the greatest challenge facing the evaluator is to integrate nomothetic findings in the case, such as scores on risk assessment scales, with idiographic data specific to the individual.

Evaluations of sexual offenders provided by mental health professionals can have a significant impact on the protection of society, as well as the protection of individual civil liberties. Although much of what is currently known about the evaluation of sexual offenders is summarized in this volume, it is by no means exhaustive. Evaluators in this arena will have to remain current in the field as the science continues to grow. We hope that this book will provide a model to assist evaluators in addressing and managing these issues.

References

Abel, G. G., Becker, J. V., Mittelman, M. S., Cunningham-Rathner, J. Rouleau, J. L., & Murphy, W. D. (1987). Self-reported sex crimes of nonincarcerated paraphiliacs. *Journal of Interpersonal Violence, 2,* 3–25.

Abel, G. G., Becker, J. V., Cunningham-Rathner, J., Mittleman, M., & Rouleau, J. L. (1988). Multiple paraphilic diagnoses among sex offenders. *Bulletin of the American Academy of Psychiatry and the Law, 16,* 153–168.

Abel, G. G., Becker, J. V., Murphy, W. D., & Flanagan, B. (1981). Identifying dangerous child molesters. In R. Stuart (Ed.), *Violent behavior: Social learning approaches to prediction, management and treatment* (pp. 116–137). New York: Brunner/Mazel.

Abel, G. G., Huffman, J., Warberg, B., & Holland, C. L. (1998). Visual reaction time and plethysmography as measures of sexual interest in child molesters. *Sexual Abuse: A Journal of Research and Treatment, 10,* 81–95.

Abel, G. G., Jordan, A. D., Hand, C. G., Holland, L. A., & Phipps, A. (2001). Classification models of child molesters utilizing the Abel assessment for sexual interest. *Child Abuse & Neglect, 25,* 703–718.

Allen, C. (1991). *Women and men who sexually abuse children: A comparative analysis.* Orwell, VT: The Safer Society Press.

Amenta, A. (2005). *The assessment of sex offenders for civil commitment proceedings: An analysis of report content.* Unpublished doctoral dissertation, Sam Houston State University, Huntsville, TX.

American Academy of Psychiatry and the Law. (2005). *Ethical guidelines for the practice in forensic psychiatry.* Retrieved January 2, 2008, from https://www.aapl.org/pdf/ETHICSGDLNS.pdf

American Psychiatric Association. (1983). Statement on the insanity defense. *American Journal of Psychiatry, 140,* 681–688.

American Psychiatric Association. (2000). *Diagnostic and statistical manual of mental disorders* (4th ed., text revision). Washington, DC: Author.

American Psychological Association (2002). The ethical principles of psychologists and code of conduct. *American Psychologist, 57,* 1060–1073.

Andrews, D. A., & Bonta, J. (2003). *The psychology of criminal conduct* (3rd ed.). Cincinnati, OH: Anderson Press.

Archer, R. P., Buffington-Vollum, J. K., Stredny, R. V., & Handel, R. W. (2006). A survey of psychological test use patterns among forensic psychologists. *Journal of Personality Assessment, 87,* 84–94.

Association for the Treatment of Sexual Abusers. (1993). *The ATSA practitioner's handbook.* Lake Oswego, OR: Author.

Association for the Treatment of Sexual Abusers (1997). *Ethical standards and principles for the management of sexual abusers.* Beaverton, OR: Author.

Association for the Treatment of Sexual Abusers. (2005). *Practice standards and guidelines.* Beaverton, OR: Author.

Bank, S. C., & Packer, I. K. (2007). Expert witness testimony: Law, ethics, and practice. In A. M. Goldstein (Ed.), *Forensic psychology: Emerging topics and expanding roles* (pp. 421–445). Hoboken, NJ: John Wiley & Sons.

Barbaree, H. E. (2005). Psychopathy, treatment behavior, and recidivism: An extended follow-up of Seto and Barbaree. *Journal of Interpersonal Violence, 20,* 1115–1131.

Barbaree, H. E., & Marshall, W. L. (1988). Deviant sexual arousal, demographic features, and offense history variables as predictors of re-offense among untreated child molesters and incest offenders. *Behavioral Sciences and the Law, 6,* 257–280.

Barbaree, H. E., & Marshall, W. L. (1989). Erectile responses among heterosexual child molesters, father–daughter incest offenders, and matched non-offenders: Five distinct age preference profiles. *Canadian Journal of Behavioural Science, 21,* 70–82.

Barbaree, H. E., & Marshall, W. L. (1998). Treatment of the sexual offender. In R. M. Wettstein (Ed.), *Treatment of offenders with mental disorders* (pp. 265–328). New York: Guilford Press.

Barbaree, H. E., Seto, M. C., Langton, C. M., & Peacock, E. J. (2001). Evaluating the predictive accuracy of six risk assessment instruments for adult sexual offenders. *Criminal Justice and Behavior, 28,* 490–521.

Barnickol, L. (2000). Missouri's Sexually Violent Predator Law: Treatment or punishment? *Journal of Law and Policy, 4,* 321–339.

Barsky, A. E., & Gould, J. W. (2002). *Clinicians in court: A guide to subpoenas, depositions, testifying, and everything else you need to know.* New York: Guilford Press.

Bartosh, D. L., Garby, T., Lewis, D., & Gray, S. (2003). Differences in predictive validity of actuarial risk assessments in relation to sex offender type. *International Journal of Offender Therapy and Comparative Criminology, 47,* 422–438.

Bauer, C. J. (2006). *A categorical analysis of Psychopathy Checklist–Revised scores in sex offenders.* Unpublished masters thesis, Sam Houston State University, Huntsville, TX.

Bechara, A., Damasio, H., & Damasio, A. R. (2000). Emotion, decision-making and the orbitofrontal cortex. *Cerebral Cortex, 10,* 295–307.

Becker, J. V., & Hunter, J. A. (1997). Understanding and treating child and adolescent sexual offenders. *Advances in Child Clinical Psychology, 19,* 177–197.

Becker, J. V., & Murphy, W. D. (1998). What we know and do not know about assessing and treating sex offenders. *Psychology, Public Policy, and Law, 4,* 116–137.

Becker, J. V., Stinson, J., Tromp, S., & Messer G. (2003). Characteristics of individuals petitioned for civil commitment. *International Journal of Offender Therapy and Criminology, 47,* 185–195.

Beech, A. R., Fisher, D. D., & Thornton, D. (2003). Risk assessment of sex offenders. *Professional Psychology: Research and Practice, 34,* 339–352.

Beech, A. R., & Ward, T. (2004). The integration of etiology and risk in sex offenders: A theoretical model. *Aggression and Violent Behavior, 10,* 31–63.

Bersoff, D. N. (Ed.) (2003). *Ethical conflicts in psychology* (3rd ed.). Washington, DC: American Psychological Association.

Bersoff, D. N., & Glass, D. J. (1995). The not-so Weisman: The Supreme Court's continuing misuse of social science research. *University of Chicago Law School Roundtable, 2,* 279–302.

Blair, R. J. R., & Ciplotti, L. (2000). Impaired social response reversal: A case of acquired sociopathy. *Brain, 123,* 1122–1141.

Boer, D. P. (2006). Sexual offender risk assessment strategies: Is there a convergence of opinion yet? *Sexual Offender Treatment, 2.* Retrieved May 7, 2008, from http://www.sexual-offender-treatment.org/38.0.html

Borum, R. (2003). Not guilty by reason of insanity. In T. Grisso. *Evaluating competencies* (2nd ed.) (pp. 193–227). New York: Kluwer Academic.

Borum, R., & Grisso, T. (1996). Establishing standards for criminal forensic reports. *Bulletin of the American Academy of Psychiatry and the Law, 15,* 297–317.

Branaman, T. F., & Gallagher S. N. (2005). Polygraph testing in sex offender treatment: A review of the limitations. *American Journal of Forensic Psychology, 23,* 45–64.

Brodsky, S. L. (1991). *Testifying in court: Guidelines and maxims for the expert witness.* Washington, DC: American Psychological Association.

Brodsky, S. L. (1999). *The expert expert witness: More maxims and guidelines for testifying in court.* Washington, DC: American Psychological Association.

Bumby, K. M., & Maddox, M. C. (1999). Judges' knowledge about sexual offenders, difficulties presiding over sexual offense cases, and opinions in sentencing, treatment, and legislation. *Sexual Abuse: A Journal of Research and Treatment, 11,* 305–315.

Burns, J. M. & Swerdlow, R. H. (2003). Right orbitofrontal tumor with pedophilia symptom and constructional apaxia sign. *Archives of Neurology, 60,* 437–440.

Bush, S. S., Connell, M. A., & Denney, R. L. (2006). *Ethical practice in forensic psychology: A systematic model for decision making.* Washington, DC: American Psychological Association.

California Department of Mental Health (2004). *Clinical evaluator handbook and standardized assessment protocol.* Sacramento, CA: Author.

Campbell, T. W. (1999). Challenging the evidentiary reliability of DSM-IV. *American Journal of Forensic Psychology, 17,* 47–68.

Campbell, T. W. (2004). *Assessing sex offenders: Problems and pitfalls.* Springfield, IL: Charles C. Thomas.

Christianson, A., & Thyer, B. (2003). Female sexual offenders: A review of empirical research. *Journal of Human Behavior in the Social Environment, 6,* 1–16.

Committee on Ethical Guidelines for Forensic Psychologists. (1991). Specialty guidelines for forensic psychologists. *Law and Human Behavior, 15,* 655–665.

Conroy, M. A. (2003). Evaluation of sexual predators. In A. M. Goldstein (Ed.), *Handbook of psychology: Forensic psychology* (Vol. 11, pp. 463–484). New York: John Wiley & Sons.

Conroy, M. A. (2006). Risk management of sexual offenders: A model for community intervention. *Journal of Psychiatry and Law, 3,* 5–23.

Conroy, M. A., & Murrie, D. C. (2007). *Forensic assessment of violence risk: A guide for risk assessment and risk management.* Hoboken, NJ: John Wiley & Sons.

Craig, L. A., Thornton, D., Beech, A., & Browne, K. D. (2007). The relationship of statistical and psychological risk markers to sexual reconviction in child molesters. *Criminal Justice and Behavior, 34,* 314–329.

Cunningham, M. D., & Reidy, T. J. (1998). Antisocial personality disorder and psychopathy: Diagnostic dilemmas in classifying patterns of antisocial behavior in sentencing evaluations. *Behavioral Sciences and the Law, 16,* 331–351.

DeClue, G. (2002). Feigning does not equal malingering. *Behavioral Sciences and the Law, 20,* 717–726.

DeClue, G. (2004, August 5). On the admissibility of testimony utilizing an aide-mémoire in a *Frye* state. *WebPsychEmpiricist.* Retrieved November 14, 2006, from http://www.wpe.info/papers_table.html

DeClue, G. (2006). What I learned about assessing people who have been convicted of sexual offenses from the Presidents of the United States of America. *Journal of Sexual Offender Civil Commitment: Science and the Law, 1,* 99–123.

de Vogel, V., de Ruiter, C., van Beek, D. & Mead, G. (2004). Predictive validity of the SVR-20 and Static-99 in a Dutch sample of treated sex offenders. *Law and Human Behavior, 28,* 235–251.

Doren, D. M. (1998). Recidivism base rates, predictions of sex offender recidivism, and the "sexual predator" commitment laws. *Behavioral Sciences and the Law, 16,* 97–114.

Doren, D. M. (2002). *Evaluating sex offenders: A manual for civil commitment and beyond.* Thousand Oaks, CA: Sage Press.

Doren, D. M. (2004). Toward a multidimensional model for sexual recidivism risk. *Journal of Interpersonal Violence, 19,* 835–856.

Doren, D. M., & Epperson, D. L. (2001). Great analysis, but problematic assumptions: A critique of Janus and Meehl (1997). *Sexual Abuse: A Journal of Research and Treatment, 13,* 45–51.

Douglas, K. S. (2007, May). *Risk assessment.* Workshop presented for the American Academy of Forensic Psychology, Ft. Lauderdale, FL.

Douglas, K. S., & Skeem, J. L. (2005). Violence risk assessment: Getting specific about being dynamic. *Psychology, Public Policy, and Law, 11,* 347–383.

Douglas, K. S., Webster, C. D., Hart, S. D., Eaves, D., & Ogloff, J. R. P. (2001). *HCR-20 Violence risk management companion guide.* Burnaby, British Columbia, Canada: Simon Fraser University, Mental Health, Law, and Policy Institute.

Dutton, W. A., & Emerick, R. L. (1996). Plethysmograph assessment. In K. English, S. Pullen, & L. Jones (Eds.), *Managing adult sex offenders: A containment approach* (pp. 14-1–14-13). Lexington, KY: American Probation and Parole Association.

Edens, J. F., Cruise, K. R., & Buffington-Vollum, J. K. (2001). Forensic and correctional applications of the Personality Assessment Inventory. *Behavioral Science and the Law, 19,* 519–543.

Edens, J. F, Marcus, D. K., Lilienfeld, S. O., & Poythress, N. G. (2006). Psychopathic, not psychopath: Taxometric evidence for the dimensional structure of psychopathy. *Journal of Abnormal Psychology, 115,* 131–44.

English, K., Pullen, S., & Jones, L. (Eds.) (1996). *Managing adult sex offenders: A containment approach.* Lexington, KY: American Probation and Parole Association.

Epperson, D. L., Kaul, J. D., & Hasselton, D. (1998, October). *Final report of the development of the Minnesota Sex Offender Screening Tool–Revised (MnSOST-R).* Presented at the 17th Annual Research and Treatment Conference of the Association for the Treatment of Sexual Abusers, Vancouver, British Columbia, Canada.

Fabian, J. M. (2005). The risky business of conducting risk assessments for those already civilly committed as sexually violent predators. *William Mitchell Law Review, 32,* 81–159.

Firestone, P., Bradford, J. M., Greenberg, D. M., & Serran, G. A. (2000). The relationship between deviant sexual arousal and psychopathy in incest offenders, extrafamilial child molesters, and rapists. *Journal of the American Academy of Psychiatry and the Law, 28,* 303–308.

Firestone, P., Bradford, J. M., McCoy, M., Greenberg, D. M., Larose, M. R., & Curry, S. (1999). Prediction of recidivism in incest offenders. *Journal of Interpersonal Violence, 14,* 511–531.

Fischer, L., & Smith, G. (1999). Statistical adequacy of the Abel Assessment for Interest in Paraphilias. *Sexual Abuse: A Journal of Research and Treatment, 11,* 195–205.

Fradella, H. F., Fogarty, A., & O'Neill, L. (2003). The impact of *Daubert* on the admissibility of behavioral science testimony. *Pepperdine Law Review,30,* 403–444.

Frenzel, R. R., & Lang, R. A. (1989). Identifying sexual preferences in intrafamilial and extrafamilial child sexual abusers. *Annals of Sex Research, 2,* 255–275.

Freund, K. & Costell, R. (1970). The structure of erotic preference in the nondeviant male. *Behavior Research and Therapy, 8,* 15–20.

Furby, L., Weinrott, M. R., & Blackshaw, L. (1989). Sex offender recidivism: A review. *Psychological Bulletin, 105,* 3–30.

Gallagher, C. A., Wilson, D. B., Hirschfield, P., Coggeshall, M. B., & MacKenzie, D. L. (1999). A quantitative review of the effects of sex offender treatment on sexual reoffending. *Corrections Management Quarterly, 3,* 19–29.

Greenberg, D., Bradford, J., Firestone, P., & Curry, S. (2000). Recidivism of childmolesters: A study of victim relationship with the perpetrator. *Child Abuse and Neglect, 24,* 1485–1494.

Greenberg, S. A., & Shuman, D.W. (1997). Irreconcilable conflict between therapeutic and forensic roles. *Professional Psychology: Research and Practice, 28,* 50–57.

Greenberg, S. A., & Shuman, D.W. (2007). When worlds collide: Therapeutic and forensic roles. *Professional Psychology: Research and Practice, 38,* 129–132.

Grisso, T. (1998). *Forensic evaluation of juveniles.* Sarasota, FL: Professional Resource Press.

Groth, A. N., Burgess, A. W., & Holmstrom, L. L. (1977). Rape: Power, anger, and sexuality. *American Journal of Psychiatry, 134,* 1239–1243.

Groth-Marnat, G. (2003). *Handbook of psychological assessment* (4th ed.). Hoboken, NJ: John Wiley & Sons.

Grove, W. M., & Meehl, P. E. (1996). Comparative efficiency of informal (subjective impressionistic) and formal (mechanical, algorithmic) prediction procedures: The clinical–statistical controversy. *Psychology, Public Policy, and Law, 2,* 293–323.

Grubin, D., & Madsen, L. (2005). Lie detection and the polygraph: A historical review. *Journal of Forensic Psychiatry and Psychology, 16,* 357–369.

Grubin, D., & Madsen, L. (2006). Accuracy and utility of post-conviction polygraph testing of sexual offenders. *British Journal of Psychiatry, 188,* 479–483.

Guay, J., Proulx, J., Cusson, M., & Ouimet, M. (2001). Victim-choice polymorphia among serious sex offenders. *Archives of Sexual Behavior, 30,* 521–533.

Hall, G. C. N. (1995). Sexual offender recidivism revisited: A meta-analysis of recent treatment studies. *Journal of Consulting and Clinical Psychology, 63,* 802–809.

Hall, G. C. N., Shondrick, D. D., & Hirschman, R. (1993). The role of sexual arousal in sexually aggressive behavior: A meta-analysis. *Journal of Consulting and Clinical Psychology, 61,* 1091–1095.

Hanson, R. K. (1998). What do we know about sex offender risk assessment? *Psychology, Public Policy, and Law, 4,* 50–72.

Hanson, R. K. (2002). Recidivism and age: Follow-up data from 4,673 sexual offenders. *Journal of Interpersonal Violence, 17,* 1046–1062.

Hanson, R. K., Broom, I., & Stephenson, M. (2004). Evaluating community sex offender treatment programs: A 12-year follow-up of 724 offenders. *Canadian Journal of Behavioural Science, 36,* 87–96.

Hanson, R. K., & Bussiere, M. T. (1998). Predicting relapse: A meta-analysis of sexual recidivism studies. *Journal of Consulting and Clinical Psychology, 66,* 348–362.

Hanson, R. K., Gordon, A., Harris, A. J. R., Marques, J. K., Murphy, W., Quinsey, V. L., & Seto, M. C. (2002). First report of the collaborative outcome data project on the effectiveness of psychological treatment for sex offenders. *Sexual Abuse: A Journal of Research and Treatment, 14,* 169–194.

Hanson, R. K., & Harris, A. J. R. (1998). *Dynamic predictors of sexual recidivism* (User Report 97-04). Ottawa, Ontario: Department of Solicitor General of Canada.

Hanson, R. K., & Harris, A. J. R. (2000). Where should we intervene? Dynamic predictors of sex offense recidivism. *Criminal Justice and Behavior, 27,* 6–35.

Hanson, R. K., & Morton-Bourgon, K. E. (2004). *Predictors of sexual recidivism: An updated meta-analysis* (Research Rep. No. 2004–02). Ottawa, Ontario: Public Safety and Emergency Preparedness Canada.

Hanson, R. K., & Morton-Bourgon, K. (2005). The characteristics of persistent sexual offenders: A meta-analysis of recidivism studies. *Journal of Consulting and Clinical Psychology, 73,* 1154–1163.

Hanson, R. K., & Thornton, D. (2000). Improving risk assessments for sex offenders: A comparison of three actuarial scales. *Law and Human Behavior, 24,* 119–136.

Hare, R. D. (1998). Psychopaths and their nature: Implications for the mental health and criminal justice systems. In T. Millon, E. Simonsen, M. Birket-Smith, & R. D. Davis (Eds.), *Psychopathy: Antisocial, criminal and violent behavior* (pp. 188–212). New York: Guilford Press.

Harris, G. T., & Rice, M. E. (1996). The science of phallometric testing of male sexual interest. *Current Directions Psychological Science, 5,* 156–160.

Harris, G. T., Rice, M. E., & Quinsey, V. L. (1998). Appraisal and management of risk in sexual aggressors: Implications for criminal justice policy. *Psychology, Public Policy, and Law, 4,* 73–115.

Harris, G. T., Rice, M. E., & Quinsey, V. L., Chaplin, T. C., & Earls, C. (1992). Maximizing the discriminant validity of phallometric assessment data. *Psychological Assessment, 4,* 502–511.

Harris, G. T., Rice, M. E., Quinsey, V. L., Lalmiere, M.L. Boer, D., & Lang, C. (2003). A multi-site comparison of actuarial risk instruments for sex offenders. *Psychological Assessment: A Journal of Consulting and Clinical Psychology, 15,* 413–425.

Heilbrun, K. (1997). Prediction versus management models relevant to risk assessment: The importance of legal decision-making context. *Law and Human Behavior, 21,* 347–359.

Heilbrun, K. (2001). *Principles of forensic mental health assessment.* New York: Kluwer Academic/Plenum Press.

Heilbrun, K., Dvoskin, J., Hart, S. D., & McNeil, D. (1999). Violence risk communication: Implications for research, policy, and practice. *Health, Risk, & Society, 1,* 91–106.

Heilbrun, K., Grisso, T., & Goldstein, A. M. (In press). *Foundations of forensic mental health assessment.* New York: Oxford University Press.

Heilbrun, K., Marczyk, G. R., & DeMatteo, D. (2002). *Forensic mental health assessment: A casebook.* New York: Oxford University Press.

Heilbrun, K., Nezu, C. M., Keeney, M., Chung, S., & Wasserman, A. L. (1998). Sexual offending: Linking assessment, intervention, and decision making. *Psychology, Public Policy, and Law, 4,* 138–174.

Heilbrun, K., O'Neill, M. L., Stevens, T. N., Strohman, L. K., Bowman, Q., & Lo, Y. (2004). Assessing normative approaches to communicating violence risk: A national survey of psychologists. *Behavioral Sciences and the Law, 22,* 187–196.

Heilbrun, K., O'Neill, M. L., Strohman, L. K., Bowman, Q., & Philipson, J. (2000). Expert approaches to communicating violence risk. *Law and Human Behavior, 24,* 137–148.

Heilbrun, K., Philipson, J., Berman, L., & Warren, J. (1999). Risk communication: Clinicians' reported approaches and perceived values. *Journal of the American Academy of Psychiatry and the Law, 27,* 397–406.

Hess, A. K. (2006). Serving as an expert witness. In I. B. Weiner & A. K. Hess (Eds.), *The handbook of forensic psychology* (3rd ed.) (pp. 652–697). Hoboken, NJ: John Wiley & Sons.

Hetzel, T. (2007). Compatibility of therapeutic and forensic roles. *Professional Psychology: Research and Practice, 28,* 122–128.

Hildebran, D. D., & Pithers, W. D. (1992). Relapse prevention: Application and outcome. In W. O'Donohue & J. H. Greer (Eds.), *The sexual abuse of children: Clinical issues* (Vol. 2, pp. 365–393). Hillsdale, NJ: Lawrence Erlbaum.

Hildebrand, M. (2004). Psychopathy and sexual deviance in treated rapists: Association with sexual and nonsexual recidivism. *Sexual Abuse: A Journal of Research and Treatment, 16,* 1–24.

Hildebrand, M., de Ruiter, C., & de Vogel, V. (2004). Psychopathy and sexual deviance in treated rapists: Association with sexual and non-sexual recidivism. *Sexual Abuse: A Journal of Research and Treatment, 16,* 1–24.

Hislop, J. (2001). *Female sex offenders.* Ravensdale, WA: Issues Press.

Hoberman, H. M. (1999). The forensic evaluation of sex offenders in civil commitment proceedings. In A. Schlank & F. Cohen (Eds.), *The sexual predator: Law, policy, evaluation, and treatment* (pp. 7-1–7-41). Kingston, NJ: Civic Research Institute.

Janus, E. S. (1998). *Hendricks* and the moral terrain of police power civil commitments. *Psychology, Public Policy and Law, 4,* 297–322.

Johansson-Love, J., & Fremouw, W. (2006). A critique of the female sexual perpetrator. *Aggression and Violent Behavior, 11,* 12–26.

Knight, R. A., Carter, D. L., & Prentky, R. A. (1989). A system for the classification of child molesters: Reliability and application. *Journal of Interpersonal Violence, 4,* 3–23.

Knight, R. A., Rosenberg, R., & Schneider, B. (1985). Classification of sexual offenders: Perspectives, methods, and validation. In A. Burgess (Ed.), *Rape and sexual assault: A research handbook* (pp. 222–293). New York: Garland Publishing.

Krauss, D. A., & Lee, D. (2003). Deliberating on dangerousness and death: Jurors ability to differentiate between expert actuarial and clinical predictions of dangerousness. *International Journal of Law and Psychiatry, 26,* 113–137.

Krauss, D. A., & Sales, B. D. (2001). The effects of clinical and scientific expert testimony on juror decision making in capital sentencing. *Psychology, Public Policy, and Law, 7,* 267–310.

Kravitz, H. M., Haywood, T. W., Kelly, J., Wahlstrom, C., Liles, S., & Cavanaugh, J. L. (1995). Medroxyprogesterone treatment for paraphilics. *Bulletin of the American Academy of Psychiatry and the Law, 23,* 19–33.

Kwartner, P. K., Lyons, P. M., & Boccaccini, M. T. (2006). Judges' risk communication preferences in risk for future violence cases. *International Journal of Forensic Mental Health, 5,* 185–194.

La Fond, J. Q. (2000). The future of involuntary civil commitment in the U.S.A. after *Kansas v. Hendricks. Behavioral Sciences and the Law, 18,* 153–167.

LaFond, J. Q. (2005). *Preventing sexual violence: How society should cope with sex offenders.* Washington, DC: American Psychological Association.

Lalumiere, M. L., & Harris, G. T. (1998). Common questions regarding the use of phallometric testing with sexual offenders. *Sexual Abuse: A Journal of Research and Treatment, 10,* 227–237.

Lalumiere, M. L., Harris, G. T., Quinsey, V. L., & Rice, M. E. (2005). *The causes of rape: Understanding individual differences in male propensity for sexual aggression.* Washington, DC: American Psychological Association.

Lalumiere, M. L., & Quinsey, V. L. (1994). The discriminability of rapists from non-sex offenders using phallometric measures: A meta-analysis. *Criminal Justice and Behavior, 21,* 150–175.

Langevin, R. Curnoe, S., Federoff, P., Bennett, R., Langevin, M., Peever, C., Pettica, R., & Sandhu, S. (2004). Lifetime sex offender recidivism: A 25-year follow-up study. *Canadian Journal of Criminology and Criminal Justice, 46,* 531–552.

Langton, C. M., Barbaree, H. E., Harkins, L., & Peacock, E. J. (2006). Sex offenders' response to treatment and its association with recidivism as a function of psychopathy. *Sexual Abuse: A Journal of Research and Treatment.* Retrieved November 10, 2007 from http://www.springer-link.com/media/012c8x61qp7rtm8arvv3/contributions

Levenson, J. S. (2004a). Reliability of sexually violent predator civil commitment criteria. *Law and Human Behavior, 28,* 357–369.

Levenson, J. S. (2004b). Sexual predator civil commitment: A comparison of selected and released offenders. *International Journal of Offender Therapy and Comparative Criminology, 48,* 638–648.

Levensen, J., & Morin, J. W. (2006). Factors predicting selection of sexually violent predators for civil commitment. *International Journal of Offender Therapy and Comparative Criminology, 50,* 609–629.

Levin, S. M., & Stava, L. (1987). Personality characteristics of sex offenders: A review. *Archives of Sexual Behavior, 16,* 57–79.

Lewis, C. F., & Stanley, C. R. (2000). Women accused of sexual offenses. *Behavioral Sciences and the Law, 18,* 73–81.

Lieb, R. (2003). State policy perspectives on sexual predator laws. In B. J. Winick & J. Q. LaFond (Eds.), *Protecting society from sexually dangerous offenders: Law, justice, and therapy.* Washington, DC: American Psychological Association.

Lilienfeld, S. O., Waldman, I. D., & Israel, A. C. (1994). A critical examination of the use of the term and concept of comorbidity in psychopathology research. *Clinical Psychology: Science and Practice, 1,* 71–83.

Lubet, S. (1998). *Expert testimony: A guide for expert witnesses and the lawyers who examine them.* Notre Dame, IN: National Institute for Trial Advocacy.

Marcus, D. K., John, S. L. & Eden, J. F. (2004). A taxometric analysis of psychopathic personality. *Journal of Abnormal Psychology, 113,* 626–635.

Marques, J. K., Wiederanders, M., Day, D. M., Nelson, C., & van Ommeren, A. (2005). Effects of a relapse prevention program on sexual recidivism: Final results from California's Sex Offender Treatment and Evaluation Project (SOTEP). *Sexual Abuse: A Journal of Research and Treatment, 17,* 79–107.

Marshall, W. L. (2006a). Appraising treatment outcome with sexual offenders. In W. L. Marshall, Y. Fernandez, L. E. Marshall, & G. A. Serran (Eds.), *Sexual offender treatment: Controversial issues* (pp. 255–274). New York: John Wiley & Sons.

Marshall, W. L. (2006b). Clinical and research limitations in the use of phallometric testing with sexual offenders. *Sexual Offender Treatment, 1,* 1–18. Retrieved May 7, 2008, from http://www.sexual-offender-treatment. org/index.php?id=18&type=123

Marshall, W. L., & Anderson D. (1996). An evaluation of the benefits of relapse prevention programs with sex offenders. *Sexual Abuse: A Journal of Research and Treatment, 3,* 499–511.

Marshall, W. L., & Fernandez, Y. M. (2000). Phallometric testing with sexual offenders: Limits to its value. *Clinical Psychology Review, 20,* 807–822.

McAllister, S. R. (1998). Sex offenders and mental illness: A lesson in federalism and the separation of powers. *Psychology, Public Policy, and Law, 4,* 268–296.

McConaghy, N. (1999). Methodological issues concerning evaluation of treatment for sexual offenders: Randomization, treatment dropouts, untreated controls, and within-treatment studies. *Sexual Abuse: A Journal of Research and Treatment, 11,* 183–194.

McGrath, R. J., Cumming, G., & Holt, J. (2002). Collaboration among sex offender treatment providers and probation and parole officers: The beliefs and behaviors of treatment providers. *Sexual Abuse: A Journal of Research and Treatment,14,* 49–65.

Melton, G. B., Petrila, J., Poythress, N. G., & Slobogin, C. (2007). *Psychological evaluations for the courts: A handbook for mental health professionals and lawyers* (3rd ed.). New York: Guilford Press.

Mercado, C. C., Bornstein, B. H., & Schopp, R. F. (2006). Decision-making about volitional impairment in sexually violent predators. *Law and Human Behavior, 30,* 587–602.

Mercado, C. C., Schopp, R. F., & Bornstein, B. H. (2005). Evaluating sex offenders under sexually violent predator laws: How might mental health professionals conceptualize the notion of volitional impairment? *Aggression and Violent Behavior, 10,* 289–309.

Meyer, W. J., Molett, M., Richards, C. D., Arnold, L., & Latham, J. (2003). Outpatient civil commitment in Texas for management and treatment of sexually violent predators: A preliminary report. *International Journal of Offender Therapy and Comparative Criminology, 47,* 396–406.

Miller, H. A., Amenta, A. E., & Conroy, M. A. (2005). Sexually violent predator evaluations: Empirical limitations, strategies for professionals, and research directions. *Law and Human Behavior, 29,* 29–54.

Miller, R. D. (1998). Forced administration of sex drive reducing medication to sex offenders: Treatment or punishment? *Psychology, Public Policy, and Law, 4,* 175–199.

Monahan, J. (1981). *Predicting violent behavior: An assessment of clinical techniques.* Beverly Hills, CA: Sage Press.

Monahan, J. (2006). A jurisprudence of risk assessment: Forecasting harm among prisoners, predators, and patients. *Virginia Law Review, 92,* 391–435.

Monahan, J., Heilbrun, K., Silver, E., Nabors, E., Bone, J., & Slovic, P. (2002). Communicating violence risk: Frequency formats, vivid outcomes, and forensic settings. *International Journal of Forensic Mental Health, 1,* 121–126.

Monahan, J., & Steadman, H. K. (1996). Violent storms and violent people: How meteorology can inform risk communication in mental health law. *American Psychologist, 51,* 931–938.

Money, J. (1986). *Lovemaps: Clinical concepts of sexual/erotic health and pathology, paraphilia, and gender transposition in childhood, adolescence, and maturity.* New York: Irvington.

Moran, P. (1999). The epidemiology of antisocial personality disorder. *Social Psychiatry and Psychiatric Epidemiology, 34,* 231–242.

Morse, S. J. (1998). Fear of danger, flight from culpability. *Psychology, Public Policy, and Law, 4,* 250–267.

Mullen, K., & Edens, J. (2008). A case law survey of the personality assessment inventory: Examining its role in civil and criminal trials. *Journal of Personality Assessment. 90,* 300–303.

Murphy, W. D., & Peters, J. M. (1992). Profiling child sexual abusers: Psychological considerations. *Criminal Justice and Behavior, 19,* 24–37.

National Institute of Corrections. (2004). *Prisoner intake systems: Assessing needs and classifying prisoners.* Washington, DC: U.S. Department of Justice.

National Research Council (2002). *The polygraph and lie detection: Review of the scientific evidence on the polygraph.* Washington, DC: The National Academies Press.

O'Donohue, W., Regev, L. G., & Hagstrom, A. (2000). Problems with the DSM-IV diagnosis of pedophilia. *Sexual Abuse: A Journal of Research and Treatment, 12,* 95–105.

Oksol, E. M., & O'Donohue, W. T. (2004). A critical analysis of the polygraph. In W. T. O'Donohue & E. R. Levensky (Eds.), *Handbook of forensic psychology: Resource for mental health and legal professionals* (pp. 601–634). New York: Elsevier Science.

Packard, R. L., & Levenson, J. S. (2006). Revisiting the reliability of diagnostic decisions in sex offender civil commitment. *Sex Offender Treatment. 1(3),* 609–629.

Porter, S., Fairweather, D., Drugge, J., Herve, H., Birt, A., & Boer, D. P. (2000). Profiles of psychopathy in incarcerated sexual offenders. *Criminal Justice and Behavior, 27*, 216–233.

Prentky, R. A., & Burgess, A. W. (2000). *Forensic management of sexual offenders.* New York: Kluwer Academic/Plenum Publishers.

Prentky, R. A., Knight, R. A., & Lee, A. F. S. (1997). Risk factors associated with recidivism among extrafamilial child molesters. *Journal of Consulting and Clinical Psychology, 65*, 141–149.

Prentky, R. A., Lee, A. F. S., Knight, R. A., & Cerce, D. (1997). Recidivism rates among child molesters and rapists: A methodological analysis. *Law and Human Behavior, 21*, 635–659.

Proulx, J., Pellerin, B., Paradis, Y., McKibben, A., Aubut, J., & Oimet, M. (1997). Static and dynamic predictors of recidivism in sexual aggressors. *Sexual Abuse: A Journal of Research and Treatment, 9*, 7–27.

Quinsey, V. L. (1986). Men who have sex with children. In D. N. Weisstub (Ed.), *Law and mental health: International perspectives* (Vol. 2, pp. 140–172). New York: Pergamon Press.

Quinsey, V. L., Harris, G. T., Rice, M. E., & Cormier, C. A. (1998). *Violent offenders: Appraising and managing risk.* Washington, DC: American Psychological Association.

Quinsey, V. L., Khanna, A., & Malcolm, B. (1998). A retrospective evaluation of the Regional Treatment Centre Sex Offender Treatment Program. *Journal of Interpersonal Violence, 13*, 621–644.

Quinsey, V. L., Lalumiere, M. L., Rice, M. E., & Harris, G. T. (1995). Predicting sexual offenses. In J. C. Campbell (Ed.), *Assessing dangerousness: Violence in sexual offenders, batterers, and child abusers* (pp. 114–137). Thousand Oaks, CA: Sage Press.

Quinsey, V. L., Rice, M. E., & Harris, G. T. (1995). Actuarial prediction of sexual recidivism. *Journal of Interpersonal Violence, 10*, 85–105.

Rasmussen, L. A. (1999). Factors related to recidivism among juvenile sexual offenders. *Sexual Abuse: A Journal of Research and Treatment, 11*, 69–86.

Redding, R. E. (1998). How common sense psychology can inform law and psycholegal research. *University of Chicago Law School Roundtable, 5*, 107–142.

Rice, M. E., & Harris, G. T. (1997). Cross validation and extension of the Violence Risk Appraisal Guide for child molesters and rapists. *Law and Human Behavior, 21*, 231–241.

Rice, M. E., & Harris, G. T. (2003). The size and sign of treatment effects in sex offenders. *Annals of the New York Academy of Science, 989*, 428–440.

Rice, M. E., Harris, G. T., & Quinsey, V. L. (1990). A follow-up of rapists assessed in a maximum security psychiatric facility. *Journal of Interpersonal Violence, 5*, 435–448.

Rice, M. E., Harris, G. T., & Quinsey, V. L. (1991). Sexual recidivism among child molesters released from a maximum security psychiatric institution. *Journal of Consulting and Clinical Psychology, 59*, 381–386.

Rogers, R. (2001). *Handbook of diagnostic and structured interviewing.* New York: Guilford Press.

Rogers, R., & Shuman, D. W. (2005). *Fundamentals of forensic practice.* New York: Springer.

Rosler, A., & Witztum, E. (2000). Pharmacology of paraphilias in the next millennium. *Behavioral Sciences and the Law, 18,* 43–56.

Sarkar, S. P. (2003). From *Hendricks* to *Crane:* The sexually violent predator trilogy and the inchoate jurisprudence of the U.S. Supreme Court. *Journal of the American Academy of Psychiatry and Law, 31,* 242–248.

Schopp, R. F., Scalora, M. J., & Pearce, M. (1999). Expert testimony and professional judgment: Psychological expertise and commitment as a sexual predator after *Hendricks. Psychology, Public Policy, and Law, 5,* 120–174.

Serin, R. C., Mailloux, D. L., & Malcolm, P. B. (2001). Psychopathy, deviant sexual arousal and recidivism among sexual offenders: A psycho-culturally determined group offense. *Journal of Interpersonal Violence, 16,* 234–246.

Seto, M. C., & Barbaree, H. E. (1999). Psychopathy, treatment behavior, and sex offender recidivism. *Journal of Interpersonal Violence, 14,* 1235–1248.

Slobogin, C. (1998). Psychiatric evidence in criminal trials: To junk or not to junk? *William and Mary Law Review, 40,* 1–56.

Slovic, P., Monahan, J., & MacGregor, D. G. (2000). Violence risk assessment and risk communication: The effects of using actual cases, providing instruction, and employing probability versus frequency formats. *Law and Human Behavior, 24,* 271–296.

Smith G., & Fischer L. (1999). Assessment of juvenile sexual offenders: Reliability and validity of the Abel Assessment for interest in paraphilias. *Sexual Abuse: A Journal of Research and Treatment, 11,* 207–216.

Sreenivasan, S., Weinberger, L. E., & Garrick, T. (2003). Expert testimony in sexually violent predator commitments: Conceptualizing legal standards of "mental disorder" and "likely to reoffend." *Journal of the American Academy of Psychiatry and the Law, 31,* 471–485.

Stadtland, C., Hollweg, M., Kleindienst, N., Dietl, J., Reich, U., & Nedopil, N. (2005). Risk assessment and prediction of violent and sexual recidivism in sex offenders: Long-term predictive validity of four risk assessment instruments. *Journal of Forensic Psychiatry and Psychology, 16,* 92–108.

Stalans, L. J. (2004). Adult sex offenders on community supervision: A review of recent assessment strategies and treatment. *Criminal Justice and Behavior, 31,* 564–608.

Strasberger, L. Gutheil, T., & Brodsky, A. (1997). On wearing two hats: Role conflict in serving as both psychotherapist and expert witness. *American Journal of Psychiatry, 154,* 448–456.

Tanford, J. A. (1990). The limits of a scientific jurisprudence: The Supreme Court and psychology. *Indiana Law Journal, 66,* 137–173.

Texas Department of Criminal Justice Programs and Services Division (2002, September). *Civil commitment.* Austin, TX: Author.

Vandiver, D., & Walker, J. (2002). Female sex offenders: An overview and analysis of 40 cases. *Criminal Justice Review, 27,* 284–300.

Walters, G. D., Duncan, S. A., & Mitchell-Perez, K. (2007). The latent structure of psychopathy: A taxometric investigation of the Psychopathy Checklist–Revised in a heterogeneous sample of male prison inmates. *Assessment, 14,* 270–278.

Walters, G. D., Gray, N. S., Jackson, R. L., Sewell, K. W., Rogers, R., Taylor, J., & Snowden, R. J. (2007). A taxometric analysis of the Psychopathy Checklist: Screening Version (PCL:SV): Further evidence of dimensionality. *Psychological Assessment, 19,* 330–339.

Weinrott, M. R., & Saylor, M. (1991). Self-report of crimes committed by sex offenders. *Journal of Interpersonal Violence, 6,* 286–300.

Wijk, A. V., Vermeiren, R., Loeber, R., Hart-kerkhoffs, L., Doreleijers, T., & Bullens, R. (2006). Juvenile sex offenders compared to non-sex offenders: A review of the literature 1995–2005. *Trauma, Violence, and Abuse, 7,* 227–243.

Wilson, R. J. (1998). Psychophysiological signs of faking in the phallometric test. *Sexual Abuse: A Journal of Research and Treatment, 10,* 113–126.

Winick, B. J. (1998). Sex offender law in the 1990s: A therapeutic jurisprudence analysis. *Psychology, Public Policy, and Law, 4,* 505–570.

Witt, P. H., & Barone, N. M. (2007). Assessing readiness for release with SVP civil commitment cases. *Sex Offender Law Report, 8,* pp. 1, 13–15.

Witt, P. H., DelRusso, J., Oppenheim, J., & Ferguson, G. (1997). Sex offender risk assessment and the law. *The Journal of Psychiatry and Law, 24,* 343–377.

Ziskin, J., & Faust, D. (1995). *Coping with psychiatric and psychological testimony* (5th ed., Vol. 1–3). Beverly Hills, CA: Law and Psychology Press.

Tests and Specialized Tools

HCR-20 (Webster, Douglas, Eaves, & Hart, 1997)
LSI-R (Andrews & Bonta, 1995)
MCMI-III (Millon, 1997)
MMPI-2 (Butcher, Dahlstrom, Graham, Tellegen, & Kaemmer, 1989)
MnSOST-R (Epperson, Hesselton, & Kaul, 1999)
PAI (Morey, 1991)
PCL-R (Hare, 2003)
RRASOR (Hanson, 1997)
SORAG (Quinsey, Harris, Rice, & Cormier, 2006)
SRA (Knight & Thornton, 2007)
SSPI (Seto & Lalumière, 2001)
Static-99 (Hanson & Thornton, 1999)
SVR–20 (Boer, Hart, Kropp, & Webster, 1997)
VRAG (Quinsey, Harris, Rice, & Cormier, 2006)

References for Tests and Specialized Tools

Andrews, D. A., & Bonta, J. (1995). *LSI-R: The Level of Service Inventory–Revised*. Toronto: Multi-Health Systems, Inc.

Boer, D., Hart, S., Kropp, R., & Webster, C. (1997). *Manual for the Sexual Violence Risk–20*. Burnaby, British Columbia, Canada: Simon Fraser University, Mental Health, Law, and Policy Institute.

Butcher, J., Dahlstrom, W., Graham, J., Tellegen, A., & Kaemmer, B. (1989). MMPI–2: *Manual for administration and scoring*. Minneapolis: University of Minnesota Press.

Epperson, D. L., Hesselton, D., & Kaul, J. D. (1999). *Minnesota Sex Offender Screening Tool-Revised (MnSOST-R): Development, performance, and recommended risk level cut scores*. Minneapolis: Minnesota Department of Corrections.

Hanson, R. K. (1997). *The development of a brief actuarial scale for sexual offense recidivism* (User Report No. 1997-04). Ottawa, Ontario: Department of the Solicitor General of Canada.

Hanson, R. K., & Thornton, D. (1999). *Static-99: Improving actuarial risk assessments for sex offenders.* (User Report 99-02). Ottawa, Ontario: Department of the Solicitor General of Canada.

Hare, R. D. (2003). *Hare Psychopathy Checklist–Revised (PCL-R)* (2nd ed.). Toronto, Ontario: Multi-Health Systems, Inc.

Knight, R. A, & Thornton, D. (2007). *Evaluating and improving risk assessment schemes for sexual recidivism: A long-term follow up of convicted sexual offenders* (Document No. 217618). Washington, DC: U.S. Department of Justice.

Millon, T. (1997). *MCMI-III manual* (2nd ed.). Minneapolis: Pearson Assessments.

Morey, L. C. (1991). *The Personality Assessment Inventory professional manual*. Odessa, FL: Professional Assessment Resources.

Quinsey, V. L., Harris, G. T., Rice, M. E., & Cormier, C. A. (2006). *Violent offenders: Appraising and managing risk* (2nd ed.). Washington, DC: American Psychological Association.

Seto, M. C., & Lalumière, M. L. (2001). A brief screening scale to identify pedophilic interests among child molesters. *Sexual Abuse: A Journal of Research and Treatment, 13,* 15–25.

Webster, C. D., Douglas, K. S., Eaves, D., & Hart, S. D. (1997). *HCR-20: Assessing risk for violence* (Version 2). Burnaby, British Columbia, Canada: Simon Fraser University, Mental Health, Law, and Policy Institute.

Cases and Statutes

Argersinger v. Hamlin, 92 S. Ct. 2006 (1972).

Barefoot v. Estelle, 463 U.S. 880 (1983).

Beasley v. Molett, 95 S.W. 3d 590 (Tex. App. 2002).

Collier v. Florida, 857 So. 2d 943 (2003).

Commitment of Sexually Violent Predators Act, Kan. Stat. Ann. Sec. 59–29a02 (2002).

Daubert v. Merrell Dow Pharmaceuticals, Inc., 509 U.S. 579 (1993).

Federal Rule of Evidence 702.

Frye v. United States, 293 Fed. 1013 (D.C. Cir. 1923).

Illinois v. Taylor, 782 N.E. 2d 920 (2002).

In re Branch, 890 So. 2d 322 (2004).

In re Commitment of R.S., 773 A. 2d 72 (2001).

In re Commitment of R.S., 801 A. 2d 219 (2002).

In re Detention of Broten, 62 P. 3d 514 (2003).

In re Detention of Hughes, 805 N.E. 2d 725 (2004).

In re Detention of Thorell, 72 P. 3d 708 (Wash. S. Ct. 2003).

In re Fisher, 164 S.W. 3d 637 (2005).

In re Gault, 87 S. Ct. 1428 (1967).

In re Mark, N.W. 2d 90 (2006).

In re the Matter of Leon G., 59 P. 3d 779 (Ariz. S. Ct. 2002).

In re the Matter of Alexander Mark Martinelli, 649 N.W. 2d 886 (Minn. App. 2002).

Kansas v. Crane, 534 U.S. 407 (2002).

Kansas v. Hendricks, 521 U.S. 346 (1997).

Kansas Stat. Ann. § 59–29a01–02 (2003 & Supp. 2004).

McKune v. Lile, 536 U.S. 24 (2002).

New Jersey Stat. Ann. § 30:4–27.26(b) (1998)

Ready v. Commonwealth, 824 N.E. 2d 474 (Mass. Ct. App. 2005).

Seling v. Young, 531 U.S. 250 (2001).

State of Minnesota ex rel. Pearson v. Probate Court, 309 U.S. 270 (1940).

United States v. Weber, F.3d, 06 Cal. Daily Op. Serv. 5211 (9th Cir. June 20, 2006).

Washington Laws § 71.09.020 (1990).

Key Terms

actuarial approach: a formal method that uses an equation, formula, or actuarial table to arrive at a probability, or expected value, of some outcome.

actuarial instrument: an instrument designed to obtain data that are scored numerically, with scores combined using an actuarial approach.

antisocial personality disorder (APD): a *DSM* diagnosis involving pervasive disregard for the rights of others and a longstanding pattern of rule-violating or law-breaking behavior, beginning by adolescence.

categorical: using categories rather than continuous numbers to describe something; for example, low, moderate, and high levels of risk.

civil commitment: the procedure in civil law by which an individual is placed in a secure setting based upon the presence of a mental disorder that causes the individual to be a danger to himself or others.

clinically adjusted actuarial: adjusting the results of an actuarial prediction through clinical judgment (which is not recommended), as contrasted with adjusting the interpretation of actuarial results (acceptable occasionally but likely to lower overall accuracy if done more than infrequently).

***Daubert* standard:** a legal test for the admissibility of scientific evidence in which the judge rules on whether the evidence is admissible, using criteria that may include whether the scientific basis for the evidence (1) has been tested or is testable, (2) has been peer reviewed, (3) has an acceptable error rate, and (4) is generally accepted in the field.

double jeopardy: the constitutional protection against being tried twice for the same crime.

dynamic risk factors: variables subject to change over time or through planned intervention that affect an individual's likelihood of some target behavior, such as violence or sexual violence.

empirical method (of scale construction): method of scale construction involving the scientific collection of data to gauge psychometric properties of items and scales, to promote the inclusion of those with acceptable properties, as contrasted with the rational method of scale construction.

Frye **standard:** a legal standard for admissibility of scientific or expert evidence, using "general acceptance in the field" as the criterion for whether the basis of the evidence is acceptable.

idiographic: data obtained through the investigation of one individual, usually the individual under consideration.

Incompetent to Stand Trial (IST): a legal determination that an individual is not able to proceed with disposition of charges because of that individual's present incapacities to understand charges or assist in his or her defense; usually due to mental illness or developmental disability.

Megan's Laws: laws named after Megan Kanka, and enacted in many jurisdictions in the United States, that require sex offenders to register with authorities following release from prison, and in some cases that citizens in the community be notified as well.

mental abnormality: in the context of SVP proceedings, this is one of a variety of similar terms—such as behavior abnormality or mental disorder—that serves as a precondition to SVP civil commitment. For the purposes of SVP commitment, it is defined in many statutes as "A congenital or acquired condition affecting the emotional or volitional capacity that predisposes the person to the commission of criminal sexual acts to a degree constituting the person a menace to the health and safety of others." (*Kansas Stat. Ann.* § 59–29a01, 2003 & Supp. 2004)

nomothetic: data obtained through the investigation of groups.

Not Guilty by Reason of Insanity (NGRI): a legal determination that an individual lacked criminal responsibility based upon the individual's mental state at the time of the offense as defined by applicable statute.

null hypothesis: the hypothesis that assumes that there is no effect of whatever variable is under consideration. One can never prove that there is no effect, but one can disprove that there is no effect.

paraphilia: disorders with the following *DSM-IV-TR* criteria:

1. Intense sexually arousing fantasies, sexual urges, or behaviors involving
2. nonhuman objects, the suffering or humiliation of one's partner, or children or other nonconsenting persons
3. that occur over a period of at least 6 months, and
4. these urges, fantasies, or behaviors cause the individual marked distress or functional impairment.

pedophilia: a paraphilia in which the focus of the individual's sexual interest is children.

penile plethysmograph: refers to the instrument used to measure either penile volume or circumference in phallometric assessment.

phallometric measure: a method of assessing male sexual arousal patterns by measuring either penile volume or circumference in response to exposure to different sexual stimuli.

psychopathy: a specific form of personality disorder, not included in the *DSM-IV-TR*, involving a callous, egocentric personality style, coupled with an impulsive, chronically antisocial lifestyle.

rational method (of scale construction): a method of scale construction involving a review of relevant theory and ideas, as contrasted with the empirical method of scale construction.

sexual psychopath laws: laws enacted by many states, beginning in the 1930s, allowing for high-risk sex offenders to be committed to special treatment facilities in lieu of incarceration.

sexual sadism: a paraphilia in which the focus of the individual's sexual interest is inflicting pain.

Sexually Violent Predator (SVP): a legal classification for sex offenders found eligible for civil commitment at the conclusion of their prison sentences.

special "repetitive-compulsive" sentencing: the form of sexual psychopath law in New Jersey in which sex offenders whose crimes resulted from volitional impairment could be sentenced to a special treatment facility.

static risk factors: variables that are historical or do not change through planned intervention and that are related to an individual's likelihood of some future activity, such as violence or sexual violence.

structured clinical guide: a list of specific factors, supported in the literature, around which to structure an assessment.

ultimate legal opinion: the legal determination to be made by the court regarding the issue before the judge (e.g., whether the individual should be civilly committed, whether the individual is competent to stand trial).

volitional impairment: an individual's substantial inability to control his or her behavior.

Index

About the Authors

Philip H. Witt, PhD, is a principal in Associates in Psychological Services, P.A., in Somerville, NJ. He is a diplomate in forensic psychology of the American Board of Professional Psychology. He performs forensic evaluations, testimony, and consultation in a wide range of civil and criminal areas, including personal injury, workplace discrimination, malpractice, criminal risk assessment, criminal and civil competencies, and sex offender assessment. He is a clinical associate professor at Robert Wood Johnson Medical School. A past president of the New Jersey Psychological Association, he was the 2001 recipient of that organization's Psychologist of the Year award. He is editor-in-chief for the *Journal of Psychiatry and Law*. He is currently president-elect of the American Academy of Forensic Psychology.

Mary Alice Conroy, PhD, is a professor and Director of Clinical Training for the Sam Houston State University Clinical Psychology Doctoral Program, which has a strong forensic emphasis. Prior to joining the SHSU faculty in 1997, she spent 20 years providing and supervising forensic services for the U.S. Bureau of Prisons. In this position, she testified in federal courts throughout the country and participated in over 1,200 assessments of violence risk. She is the founder and original director of the Forensic Practice Division of the Texas Psychological Association. As president of the American Academy of Forensic Psychology (2007–2009), she holds a diplomate in forensic psychology.